A NATION TORN
The Story of How the Civil War Began

"A wonderful introduction to the events that led up to America's Civil War. Ray successfully puts the confusing events of 1860 and 1861 into clear focus and, by using primary-source material, adds a human perspective."

—*School Library Journal*, starred review

"Expertly crafted . . . An excellent choice of facts and a smooth flowing narrative."   —*The Horn Book*

"[A] pleasingly designed history . . . recounted in smooth prose that's well supported with black-and-white reproductions of many photographs, drawings, and other documents of the time. . . . Civil War buffs and students needing report material will find this highly useful."   —*Booklist*

"*A Nation Torn: The Story of How the Civil War Began* and *Behind the Blue and Gray: The Soldier's Life in the Civil War* [also by Delia Ray] are masterful combinations of well researched facts, excerpts from primary sources, and period photographs. Though nonfiction, both books are well told stories that will engage young readers."   —*The Reading Teacher* (IRA)

Fort Sumter, the first battleground of the Civil War

A NATION TORN

★ ★ ★ ★

THE STORY OF HOW THE CIVIL WAR BEGAN

Delia Ray

PUFFIN BOOKS

PUFFIN BOOKS
Published by the Penguin Group
Penguin Books USA Inc., 375 Hudson Street, New York, New York 10014, U.S.A.
Penguin Books Ltd, 27 Wrights Lane, London W8 5TZ, England
Penguin Books Australia Ltd, Ringwood, Victoria, Australia
Penguin Books Canada Ltd, 10 Alcorn Avenue, Toronto, Ontario, Canada M4V 3B2
Penguin Books (N.Z.) Ltd, 182-190 Wairau Road, Auckland 10, New Zealand

Penguin Books Ltd, Registered Offices: Harmondsworth, Middlesex, England

First published in the United States of America by Lodestar Books,
an affiliate of Dutton Children's Books, a division of Penguin Books USA Inc., 1990
Published in Puffin Books, 1996

10 9 8 7 6 5 4 3 2 1

THE LIBRARY OF CONGRESS HAS CATALOGED THE LODESTAR EDITION AS FOLLOWS:
Ray, Delia.
A nation torn: the story of how the Civil War began / Delia Ray.
—1st ed.
   p. cm. — (Young readers' history of the Civil War)
Includes bibliographical references.
ISBN 0-525-67308-3
1. United States—History—Civil War, 1861–1865—Causes—Juvenile literature. 2. United States—
Politics and government—1815–1861— Juvenile literature. I. Title. II. Series.
E468.9.R39 1990
973.7'11—dc20 90-5533 CIP

Puffin Books ISBN 0-14-038105-8

Printed in the United States of America

for Caroline,
who kicked and hiccupped
through every word

Contents

★ ★ ★ ★

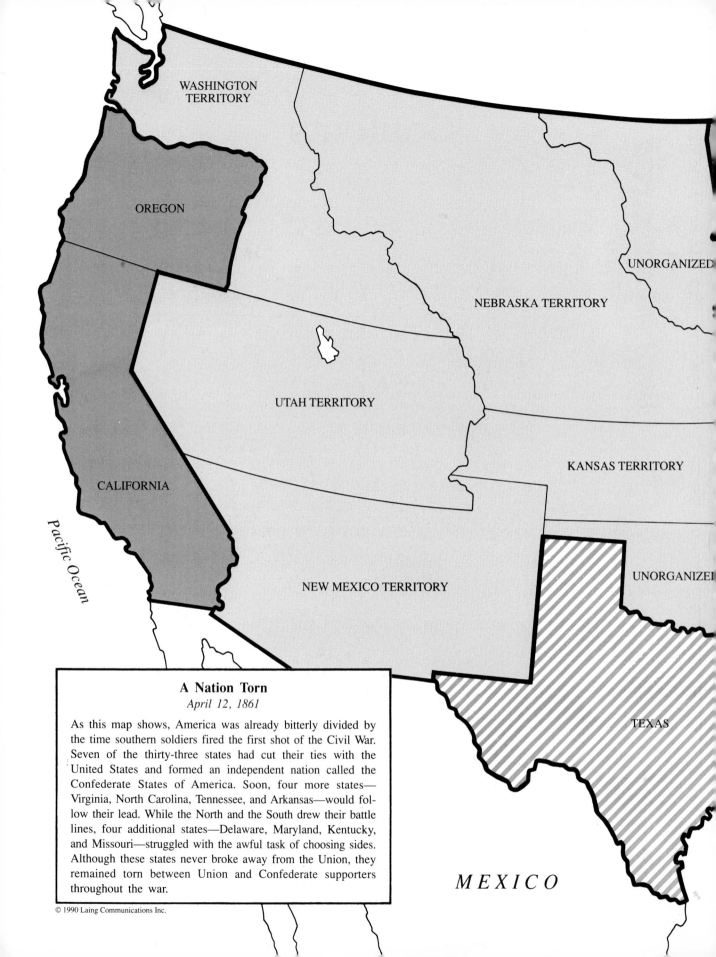

WASHINGTON
TERRITORY

OREGON

UNORGANIZED

NEBRASKA TERRITORY

UTAH TERRITORY

CALIFORNIA

Pacific Ocean

KANSAS TERRITORY

NEW MEXICO TERRITORY

UNORGANIZED

TEXAS

MEXICO

A Nation Torn
April 12, 1861

As this map shows, America was already bitterly divided by the time southern soldiers fired the first shot of the Civil War. Seven of the thirty-three states had cut their ties with the United States and formed an independent nation called the Confederate States of America. Soon, four more states—Virginia, North Carolina, Tennessee, and Arkansas—would follow their lead. While the North and the South drew their battle lines, four additional states—Delaware, Maryland, Kentucky, and Missouri—struggled with the awful task of choosing sides. Although these states never broke away from the Union, they remained torn between Union and Confederate supporters throughout the war.

CANADA

MINNESOTA

WISCONSIN

MICHIGAN

MAINE

VERMONT

NEW HAMPSHIRE

MASSACHUSETTS

NEW YORK

RHODE ISLAND

CONNECTICUT

IOWA

PENNSYLVANIA

NEW JERSEY

ILLINOIS

INDIANA

OHIO

DELAWARE

Washington, D.C.

MARYLAND

MISSOURI

VIRGINIA

KENTUCKY

Atlantic Ocean

NORTH CAROLINA

TENNESSEE

ARKANSAS

SOUTH CAROLINA

Charleston

Ft. Sumter

MISSISSIPPI

ALABAMA

GEORGIA

LOUISIANA

Free States

Slave States

Confederate States
April 12, 1861

Territories

FLORIDA

Gulf of Mexico

When Major Robert Anderson took command of the Union forces in Charleston harbor, he said good-bye to the outside world for five anxious months. During this time southern leaders periodically cut off mail delivery to the federal fort. Weeks would pass when Anderson could not communicate with his family.

ONE

A Storm in the Harbor

★ ★ ★ ★

On Christmas day in 1860, Major Robert Anderson of the United States Army wrote his wife a letter from his damp and drafty quarters many miles from home. "I am sorry to have no Christmas gift to offer you," he wrote. "Never mind—the day may *very* soon come when I shall do something which will . . . make amends."

It was impossible for Major Anderson to buy his wife a gift. For six weeks he had served as commander of Fort Moultrie, a weather-beaten brick structure on an island just off the harbor of Charleston, South Carolina. During those weeks Anderson rarely dared to leave Sullivan's Island. It was his duty to guard all the forts in the harbor from enemy attack.

The fortresses had originally been built to protect the city of Charleston from an invasion by sea. During the Revolutionary War, American soldiers bravely defended Fort Moultrie against gunfire from a fleet of British ships. But on this Christmas day, almost one hundred years later, the threat of attack came from the banks of Charleston—from an enemy that was not even foreign. Major Anderson and his small troop of soldiers were preparing to fight their own countrymen. The Americans on the shore were Southerners who, only five days earlier, had decided to turn their backs on the United States and create an independent nation.

Although Major Anderson was a loyal American who desperately wanted to keep peace between the states, he felt uneasy about his assignment at Fort Moultrie. Now that the people of South Carolina had decided to set up their own nation, they were anxious to remove all signs of the United States government from their territory, including the red, white, and blue flag that flew over Fort Moultrie. The leaders of South Carolina were determined to make Anderson and his men leave Charleston harbor. But federal officials in Washington, D.C., had ordered the major to hold his ground.

To make matters worse for Anderson, all three forts that he commanded were weak and undermanned. Fort Moultrie was the only one occupied by a regiment of soldiers. Yet there were not even enough men at Moultrie to repair the crumbling fortress, much less fight off a strong army of southern patriots.

Major Anderson's small crew of laborers worked feverishly to prepare the fort for battle, but each day their efforts seemed more and more hopeless. The brick walls were so full of gaps that enemy forces could easily invade the fort at any time. Even more disturbing, Fort Moultrie was surrounded by high sand hills and rooftops—perfect places for sharpshooters to stand and fire on the Union soldiers below.

By Christmas, Anderson had sent several letters to Washington urgently asking for more troops and further instructions, but his superiors were strangely slow to respond. At the U.S. Capitol, politicians and military leaders argued endlessly over the problem in South Carolina. They feared that any efforts to strengthen the forts would anger the rebels into starting a war. Finally, Major Anderson could wait no longer. Frustrated with the lack of guidance from his government, he decided to act on his own.

For weeks Anderson had been staring across the channel at Fort Sumter—a bleak-looking stronghold that rose out of the water in an enormous, five-sided mound. Built on a man-made island of stone blocks, the fort was surely the safest spot in the harbor. It held a commanding view of the entire area and had walls that reached fifty feet high. Anderson knew that if he could only move his garrison to Fort Sumter, he might be able to gain control of

During the mid-1800s, the city of Charleston, South Carolina, was a gathering place for citizens who wanted to rebel against the United States government and form a separate southern nation.

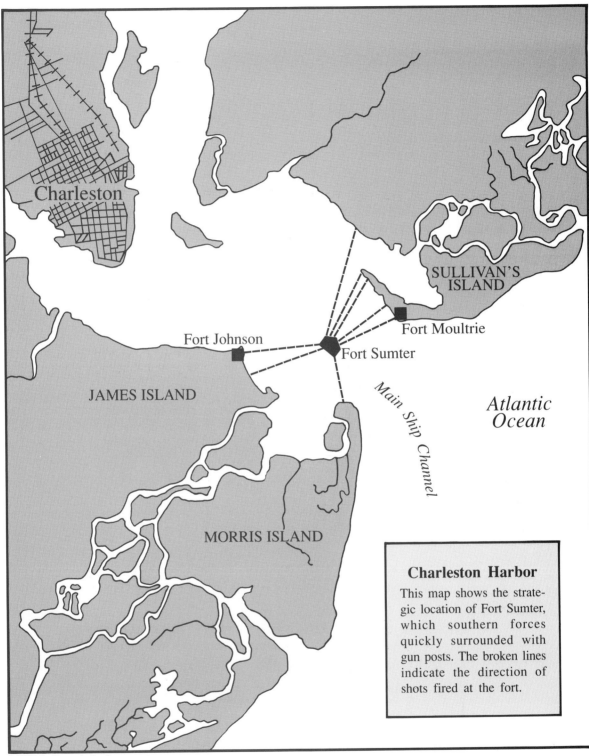

Fort Johnson

Fort Sumter

Fort Moultrie

SULLIVAN'S
ISLAND

Charleston

JAMES ISLAND

MORRIS ISLAND

Main Ship Channel

*Atlantic
Ocean*

Charleston Harbor

This map shows the strategic location of Fort Sumter, which southern forces quickly surrounded with gun posts. The broken lines indicate the direction of shots fired at the fort.

the harbor and guarantee the safety of his men. He began to make careful plans as he paced along the high parapet during the day and lay awake in his quarters at night.

Anderson could not warn even his most trusted officers of his scheme. And he could only hint at his mysterious plans in the Christmas letter to his wife, Eliza. The move had to remain a complete surprise until the last moment. If the rebels somehow learned of the plot, they might seize Fort Sumter for themselves or, much worse, open fire on Anderson's troops.

On December 26, Anderson finally revealed the secret to his men. The garrison would evacuate Fort Moultrie that evening, between five and six o'clock, just after the sun had set.

While Major Anderson's officers were startled to hear of this dangerous mission on such short notice, they prepared for the crossing with amazing speed. Captain Abner Doubleday was given just twenty minutes to organize his company of soldiers. During the rush he also had to arrange for the safety of his wife, the only woman in Fort Moultrie at the time. Doubleday warned her to leave the fort quickly, to hide behind the sand hills if firing broke out, and to take refuge with one of the families living nearby. "We took a sad and hasty leave of each other," Doubleday wrote in an account of his experiences, "for neither knew when or where we would meet again. [Then] I strapped on my revolver, tied a blanket across my shoulders, and reported to Major Anderson that my men were in readiness to move."

Once all the officers and their companies had assembled, Anderson led them out of the fort's main gates. Dusk was just beginning to fall as the soldiers marched silently along the beach facing Sumter. At each step, Anderson waited for an enemy guard to stop his men or an unfriendly passerby to cry out in alarm, but surprisingly, no one noticed the Union garrison.

A quarter of a mile down the beach, three large, six-oared boats were waiting behind a high pile of rocks. The men quickly took their places at the oars. Major Anderson pushed off in the first boat and Lieutenant Richard Meade followed in the second, leaving Doubleday to bring up the rear.

By now, a bright, full moon had risen over the harbor. As the officers scanned the stretch of water before them, they spotted one of the enemy's patrol boats, the *Nina*, puffing down the channel from Charleston. Anderson and Meade made wide circles in their vessels to avoid the patrol boat. Doubleday, however, instructed his oarsmen to row directly toward Sumter, hoping that there would be time to pass safely in front of the steamer without being observed.

Unfortunately, the soldiers on board were not experienced seamen. They handled their oars stiffly as if they were paddling with heavy logs. Doubleday's heart froze as he realized his boat was

From its strategic location at the entrance of the harbor, Fort Sumter offered a clear shot at the three enemy strongholds surrounding the channel. But Major Anderson had only sixty-eight soldiers to fight against an army of six thousand.

bound to be spotted. Quickly, he ordered his men to take off their coats and use them to cover their muskets. Even in the dim light, the Southerners would recognize the uniforms of the United States Army—long coats with shiny brass buttons and wide black hats with the right brims upturned. The captain threw off his own plumed hat and pushed open his coat to hide the gleaming buttons. He hoped that the guards would mistake the Union soldiers for a party of friendly workmen.

There was nothing else Captain Doubleday or his company could do as they breathlessly watched the *Nina* edge closer and its paddle wheels roll to a standstill. "The paddle wheels stopped within about a hundred yards of us," Doubleday later described, "but, to our great relief, after a slight scrutiny, the steamer kept on its way."

The next morning, when the *Nina* steamed past Sumter, her crew must have stared in surprise. For there, gathered along the fort's highest walls, were Major Robert Anderson's soldiers, gazing down at the passing guard boat with triumphant grins. The *Nina* rushed back to Charleston. Messengers were sent to all corners of the city to spread the alarming news: Fort Sumter was full of federal soldiers!

Once the excitement of the morning had passed, Anderson turned his attention to a more solemn duty. The major, a deeply religious man, believed that God was responsible for safely guiding his troops to Fort Sumter. To show his devotion, Anderson called the entire garrison to the courtyard for a special ceremony of thanksgiving and prayer. The soldiers stood smartly at attention as the major marched into the parade ground, proudly carrying the folded garrison flag. Then, while the chaplain prayed that the country would soon be reunited, Anderson knelt and bowed his gray head.

The men were filled with admiration for their leader. To them, Anderson was the model of a daring officer, a loyal soldier, and an honorable man. Now that they were safely within the high walls of Sumter, surrounded by the sea, the troops felt a new confidence in their country and their commander. When Anderson hoisted the flag upward, the men broke into loud, patriotic cheers for the major and the Stars and Stripes he raised.

Despite the high morale of the soldiers, the troubles at Fort

On the evening of December 26, 1860, the Union garrison secretly evacuated Fort Moultrie. To prevent the rebels from later using the weapons at Moultrie, eleven soldiers were left behind to destroy all of the cannon and set fire to the wooden gun carriages.

As the United States flag is raised, Major Anderson kneels and joins his men in a prayer of thanksgiving for the garrison's safe crossing from Fort Moultrie.

Sumter were far from over. Anderson had never meant for his move to challenge or threaten Charleston. Instead, he hoped that a stronger Union position would prevent or at least delay a terrible conflict. But the leaders of South Carolina were outraged. Convinced that Anderson's move was an act of aggression, they sent troops to seize Fort Moultrie and occupy posts all around the harbor.

Support for South Carolina was growing throughout the South at an alarming rate. By February, six other states—Mississippi, Florida, Alabama, Georgia, Louisiana, and Texas—had left the Union. On February 8, delegates from these states stunned loyal Americans when they met in Alabama to organize their new nation, which they called the Confederate States of America.

Anderson's worries mounted as the Confederacy grew in power and size. Although Sumter was the safest site in the harbor, Anderson quickly realized that this fort also had its drawbacks. For one, Sumter had never been completed. There were still walls to construct, cannon to mount, and shambles of equipment and supplies to clear from the parade ground. And, even worse, the major still had just sixty-eight soldiers and eight officers to defend his fort—a stronghold that was designed for a fighting force of six hundred and fifty men.

In March, Anderson regained hope when Abraham Lincoln became the new president of the United States. On the day he took office, Lincoln gave an unyielding speech, warning that he would do everything in his power to "hold, occupy, and possess" federal property that lay in Confederate territory. Clearly, the president was referring to Fort Sumter. But, as day after day passed without word from Washington, Anderson began to doubt whether Lincoln would ever turn his promise into action.

Meanwhile, the garrison in Charleston harbor was running out of food. Confederate authorities had cut off the fort's supply of fresh vegetables and meat. Now the garrison lived on a dismal diet of salt pork that had been pickled in barrels of vinegar. When the pork began to run low, the soldiers were reduced to rations of just two crackers a day, one in the morning and one at night.

Sick with hunger and boredom, the men began to feel abandoned by their country—like prisoners in a lonely fortress, instead of proud soldiers defending their flag. "The major is very greatly

Abner Doubleday, the tall, burly New Yorker who was second in command at Fort Sumter

depressed in spirits, and today told me he thought of taking down our flag," wrote one officer in his diary. "Without supplies, without encouragement, we are left to ourselves, and the greatest depression prevails among us."

Anderson's first instructions from the new government finally arrived on April 8. The major, who had been prepared to evacuate Sumter at any moment, was shaken by the news: The president was sending ships loaded with supplies to strengthen the fort. Hoping to avoid a clash with the Confederates, Lincoln also sent a letter to the governor of South Carolina informing him of the expedition. He assured the governor that his naval officers would unload provisions only. No soldiers or weapons would be landed unless the relief ships were attacked.

The leaders of the Confederacy did not react as Lincoln had planned. They not only wanted to block the relief mission, they wanted to clear their harbor of all Union soldiers immediately. Jefferson Davis, the president of the Confederate States of America, ordered the commander of the southern forces to take possession of Sumter. On April 11, General Pierre Gustave Toutant Beauregard sent a message to Major Anderson demanding that he remove his flag and his men from Charleston harbor.

While Beauregard's messengers waited for a reply, Anderson summoned his officers into another room to discuss the Confederacy's demand. By now, the men were well aware of the forces building against them. Each day the officers looked out at the marshes, where they could see the Confederates' sandbag barricades growing and the black metal of more and more weapons glinting in the sun. Thousands of fresh troops surrounded their weakened regiment of sixty-eight soldiers. Yet, when the officers voted on how to proceed, the decision was unanimous. The Union garrison would refuse to surrender.

As Anderson escorted the messengers out to the wharf, he informed them that he could not abandon his post. He added, however, that if the relief ships did not arrive, his garrison would be "starved out" in a few days. General Beauregard was not willing to wait for the Union soldiers' last cracker to disappear. He notified Major Anderson that the Confederates would open fire in precisely one hour.

Jefferson Davis, the president of the Confederate States of America. Before joining the Confederacy, Davis had been a prominent figure in the U.S. government, serving as a congressman, senator, and secretary of war.

General P. G. T. Beauregard, the commander of the Confederate forces at Charleston. As a young man, this handsome and dashing leader attended the U.S. Military Academy at West Point. One of his instructors at the academy had been Robert Anderson, the man who now opposed him from across the harbor.

Early in the morning on April 12, 1861, the silence over the dark harbor was split by the roar of a signal shot. Several Union officers were standing on the parapet, squinting into the blackness, when a flash of flame reddened the sky. They watched a shell from the enemy's cannon soar high over the water, spitting sparks like a rocket. Major Anderson braced himself as the shell exploded almost directly over Fort Sumter. The Civil War had begun. ★

One of the busiest streets in the world, New York City's Broadway bustled with people and traffic. In the mid-1800s, this scene became more and more typical of the thriving, industrialized life in the North.

America, North and South

★　★　★　★

When war broke out at Fort Sumter, many Americans did not know whether to shake their heads in sadness or sigh with relief. Civil war meant that the United States had truly split apart, that fellow Americans would become fierce enemies. But civil war might also bring an end to the long argument between the North and the South. The two sections of the country had been quarreling for years. Now, the waiting was finally over. The firing on Fort Sumter hit like a thunderstorm after months of dark, threatening clouds.

While the years leading up to the Civil War were uneasy, they were also a time of tremendous growth for the United States. In 1800 only eight million people lived in America. By the time the first shot exploded over Sumter, sixty years later, the number of Americans had soared to thirty-one million. The country had also added vast new territories to its borders. Miles of railroad track were built so settlers could travel to these untamed lands. And leaders in strong foreign nations such as England and France were finally beginning to pay close attention to this thriving young country.

Although growth brought the United States wealth and glory,

it also created conflicts throughout the nation. As the country changed, two very different ways of life developed within its borders—one in the North and the other in the South. The more America prospered, the more divided these two sections became.

William Howard Russell, a British newspaper reporter, traveled from England to America in 1861 to write about the changes happening on the other side of the Atlantic Ocean. His first stop was New York City. As Russell's steamship entered the harbor, he immediately noticed a whirlwind of activity along the shores. Enormous ferryboats and freighters nosed back and forth in the bay. In the distance, Russell could see the tall, blackened smokestacks of factories, where railroad parts, machinery, and other metal goods were made.

During the 1850s, the boom in railroad construction transformed the landscape of the nation as well as American life. The new railroad line from New York to Chicago, for example, cut travel time from three weeks to two days.

In the cities of the North, factories such as this tool-making operation in Vermont used power-driven machinery to manufacture products. In the South, blacksmiths still forged tools by hand.

When the steamship moved close to the dock, Russell could pick out voices in the bustling crowd. Many spoke with strange accents or called out in foreign languages. "These are all Irish and Germans," a man standing next to Russell explained. "I'll bet fifty dollars there's not a native-born American among them." It was true that most of the people on the dock were newcomers to the United States. During the mid-1800s, millions of men and women from foreign countries poured into America to find jobs in the busy mills and factories.

All across the North, cities followed New York's lead. They eagerly charged into this period of growth known as the Industrial Age. In Boston and Philadelphia, factories rose up along the streets, spewing clouds of smoke into the sky. Inventors developed new machines that turned out products at record-breaking speeds. With the flood of foreign immigrants in the North, sleepy towns such as Chicago, Illinois, seemed to expand into noisy cities in a matter of months.

When William Russell traveled to the southern states, he discovered quite a different scene. From his train window, the reporter gazed out at miles of farmland and rode for long stretches before passing a village or town. The largest city Russell visited was New Orleans, Louisiana, with a population of 150,000 people. Yet compared to the booming industrial centers of the North, New Orleans seemed small, with very few immigrants and little manufacturing. Life in the South revolved around huge estates called plantations, where sprawling fields of cotton, tobacco, and other crops were grown.

When Northerners traveled through the South, they were often struck by the small number of towns and the peacefulness of communities such as Petersburg, Virginia, shown here. One visitor commented: "From the quiet appearance of their towns, the stranger would think business was taking a siesta."

During his journey through the United States, Russell learned that the people in the two sections were as different as their cities and towns. In the North, he heard politicians and merchants accuse Southerners of being backward and old-fashioned. In the South, men called the Northerners "miserable Yankees" and complained of northern greed. Both sides often spoke as if each half of America could get along perfectly well without the other. But, in reality, the North and the South depended on each other in many ways.

One of the most important ties between the two sections was trade. The North relied on the rich fields of the South to provide raw materials for its factories. And without many factories of its own, the South had to send most of its crops north to be processed. As Russell quickly realized, this situation often caused bitter feelings, mainly in the South. Southern farmers grew furious when they described the story of their cotton. Each harvest season, they sent bales of cotton from their fields to northern mills to be made into cloth. According to the planters, the price that the merchants paid for these crops was far too low. To make matters worse, Southerners were forced to buy cloth and other factory-made goods they needed from the North for prices that seemed far too high.

The planters also traded with foreign countries such as England. But without help from the North, there was no way for them to send their tobacco, rice, and cotton overseas. America's busiest seaports and shipyards were located in the North. Businessmen there not only organized most foreign trade deals, but they owned the vessels that shipped the goods abroad. Once again, the South had to pay whatever fees the northern merchants decided to charge for their services.

The people in the South watched the North grow more and more powerful. Soon, they began to fear that the Yankees would take control of the national government and pass laws that would hurt their states' economies. John C. Calhoun, a southern senator who became vice president, was one of the first leaders in the country to foresee this danger. In 1828, Calhoun spent most of the summer alone at his plantation in South Carolina, designing a plan that would prevent the North from taking control. By the end of the summer, he was eager to spread his views.

Calhoun wanted to convince his fellow politicians that the

At the Wall Street Ferry House in New York, tall-masted clipper ships lined the docks. Many of these vessels carried cotton overseas, where northern merchants sold it at a high profit.

John C. Calhoun, a stern defender of southern rights

greatest powers should be placed in the hands of the states—not the national government in Washington, D.C. He argued that if state leaders believed a federal law was unfair, they should be allowed to change or ignore that rule within their state's borders.

Calhoun's proposal for states' rights did not meet with the approval he had hoped. It alarmed the Northerners and angered President Andrew Jackson, who saw these ideas as a threat to national unity. But support for Calhoun's program gradually spread throughout the southern states, adding more poison to the quarrels between the North and the South.

Trade and states' rights were not the only issues that drove the two sections apart. As one observer remarked, "The North and the South are two different nations in every respect, alike in one point only, their hatred for each other." For generations, people from the North and South had been developing different ways of living and thinking. Yet nothing did more to stir anger between Northerners and Southerners than the subject of slavery.

William Russell, the British reporter, was eager to investigate slavery in America. The blacks he met in New York and other northern states, however, were not slaves. The ownership of human beings had been outlawed in the North for many years. But as soon as Russell crossed into the southern states, he saw signs of slavery everywhere. In the town squares, there were auction blocks where black people were bought and sold like cattle. Behind the planters' fine houses stood rows of dirt-floored huts where slaves lived, sometimes twelve to a room.

Early one evening on the streets of Charleston, Russell heard a bell begin to toll. As the deep chimes echoed through the city, he asked his companion what the ringing meant. "It's for all the colored people to clear out of the streets and go home," the friend explained. "The guards will arrest any who are found without passes

The slave trade was a profitable business in the South, and each town usually had several dealers. Inside this market in Alexandria, Virginia, slaves were kept in pens until they were bought or sold.

At slave sales in the South, the auctioneers forced blacks to display their worth by walking back and forth in front of an audience of whites. Interested buyers often examined the slaves' teeth or felt their muscles as if they were inspecting livestock.

in half an hour." The southern whites were desperately afraid to let their slaves come and go as they pleased. They knew their fortunes would crumble unless they could keep their slaves on the plantations.

During the mid-1800s slaves in the United States numbered in the millions. In South Carolina, slaves actually outnumbered whites. But at one time, blacks were a rare sight in America. The first blacks arrived in 1619 when a Dutch ship landed on the shores of Jamestown, Virginia, and unloaded twenty Africans. Over the next two hundred years, thousands of Africans were captured from their homeland and forced to make the same dreadful voyage into slavery. Taken on board ships, the naked slaves were chained together on bare wooden boards in the lower decks, and packed so tightly that they could barely move. Many died of disease during the brutal trip across the Atlantic Ocean, which often lasted for more than three months.

Although slaves continued to arrive from Africa during the late 1700s, many Americans suspected the days of slavery were

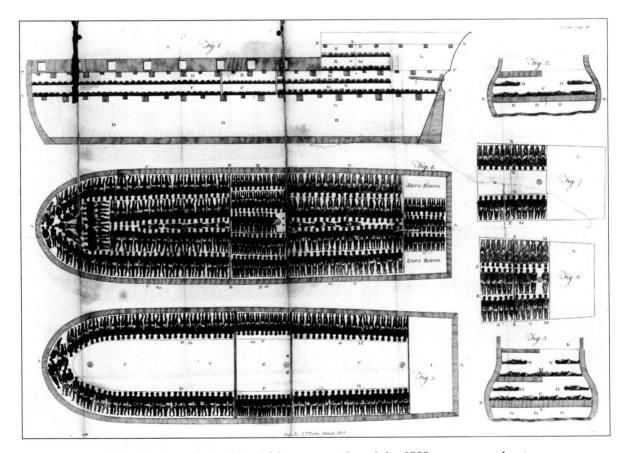

Although slave trade with Africa was outlawed in 1808, some merchants continued the practice illegally. This drawing shows how hundreds of Africans were packed into the lower decks of slave ships for an agonizing voyage across the Atlantic Ocean.

coming to an end. The practice was fading quickly in the North. With its long winters and rocky hills, the North was more suited to factories than farming. Instead of slaves, businessmen preferred immigrant workers, whom they could hire and fire as the luck of their companies changed.

In the South, slaves still toiled in fields of tobacco, rice, and cotton. But these crops did not always bring in enough money to cover the costs of feeding and housing the black workers. Some Southerners began to consider the prospect of freeing their slaves. Then, in 1793, a Yankee named Eli Whitney invented a device called the cotton gin, which changed the plantation owners' minds. During a stay in the South, Whitney had watched the slaves working at the tedious job of separating the fleecy tufts of cotton from their hard seeds. Ordinarily, it took a slave ten hours to pull the seeds from just one pound of cotton. But with Whitney's invention, up to one thousand pounds of clean fiber could be produced each day. The gin made it profitable to grow large cotton crops. Many farmers now ordered all of their slaves to pick cotton, trying to match the pace of these new machines.

The world had a huge appetite for cotton and the cloth it produced. England was hungry for as many bales of the fiber as America could send. Before long, Southerners had planted cotton on every spare acre, and they anxiously looked for new areas to spread their seeds. As their cotton kingdom grew, plantation owners bought more and more slaves to work the fields. Soon the idea of ending slavery slipped from their minds.

Although southern planters could not have built their cotton kingdom without slaves, many treated their servants worse than their animals. One slave, Solomon Northup, worked on a plantation where black workers faced cruelty and humiliation every day of their lives. Northup was more shocked than his fellow slaves by the white man's brutality. Most of the men and women who bent beside him in the cotton fields had grown up with this treatment and had worked under the overseer's whip since the age of twelve. Northup, however, did not become a slave until he was thirty-two. Born a free citizen in the state of New York, he had been kidnapped and sold into slavery in the South. He suddenly found himself on a plantation in Louisiana, forced to call another man "master."

If the slaves slackened the pace of their picking in the cotton fields, an overseer was always there to speed them along with a shout or a crack of the whip.

Northup quickly learned that the days of a slave were long and filled with back-breaking work. "The hands are required to be in the cotton field as soon as it is light in the morning," he later wrote. "With the exception of ten or fifteen minutes, which is given them at noon to swallow their . . . cold bacon, they are not permitted to be a moment idle until it is too dark to see. . . . When the moon is full, they often times labor till the middle of the night."

Even when the overseer finally called "halt" to the picking, many slaves still faced the most dreaded chore of the day. Every evening the field workers carried their baskets of cotton to the gin-house to be weighed. On Master Epps's plantation, where Northup worked, those who had not picked their full share of cotton were viciously whipped. As Northup described, "The crack of the lash, and the shrieking of the slaves, can be heard from dark till bed time on Epps's plantation, any day almost during the entire period of the cotton-picking season."

Although it was dark when the field hands returned to their

On plantations without mechanical cotton gins, slaves had to work long hours pulling seeds from the cotton by hand.

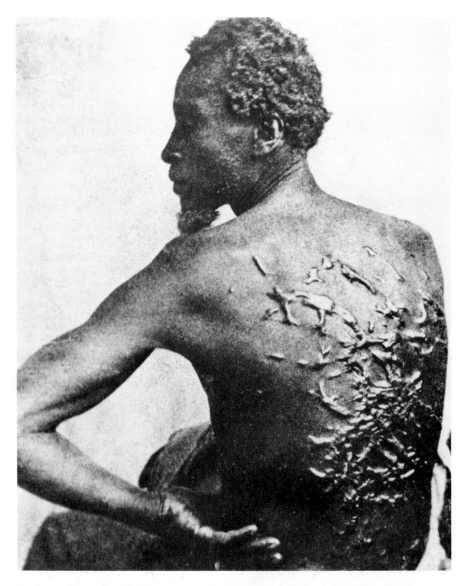

A slave shows the hideous scars of a brutal whipping. Southern landowners sometimes paid professional slave breakers to come to their plantations and whip disobedient blacks.

quarters, the evening hours were often the only time for household chores. By candlelight, the exhausted slaves fed the livestock, cut wood, and built fires in their cabins. Only then could they settle down to their meager meals of boiled cornmeal and salted bacon.

Northup fascinated his companions with stories of his old life in New York—the pleasures of raising a family, owning a home, and reading books. Many slaves spent almost every waking moment dreaming of freedom. But while Northup was rescued from slavery after twelve years of bondage, most of the blacks he met in the South remained slaves until they died.

Many plantation owners also forced young slave children to work from morning until bedtime. Booker T. Washington, who became famous as a black leader and educator, wrote of his childhood experiences in slavery. Before he reached the age of ten, Washington was hard at work on his master's farm. Each day he cleaned the yards, brought water to the field hands, and carried heavy bags of corn to the mill to be ground. "There was no period of my life that was devoted to play," Washington later wrote in his autobiography. "Almost every day . . . has been occupied in some kind of labor."

If the slaves did find a precious bit of spare time, there were strict limits on how they could spend it. In the South, it was illegal for blacks to attend school, own property, or earn money. Slaves could not even marry without their owner's permission. Those who married and had children lived in fear that their loved ones could be sold off to other plantations at any time.

For blacks, each chore was a cruel reminder of the unfair differences between their lives and those of their masters. On the Virginia farm, young Booker T. Washington was required to report to the "big house" at dinnertime to fan flies away from the table for hours as the plantation owner's family ate. From his corner of the room, Washington watched the fine food being passed around the table and listened to the conversations of life in freedom.

Washington was also ordered to follow his master's young daughter to school, carrying her books. He could walk only as far as the schoolhouse door. Slaves were not allowed inside. But through the open doorway, Washington could see several boys and girls his age studying their lessons and reading books. He yearned to join them. "I had the feeling," Washington later recalled, "that to get into a schoolhouse and study in this way would be about the same as getting into paradise."

Fortunately, the hardships of blacks were not entirely ignored. All over the North, and in hidden pockets of the South, men and women were forming groups to protest against slavery. The strong-est supporters of the antislavery cause were known as abolitionists. These people wanted the country to abolish or outlaw slavery. To promote their cause, they held meetings and published pamphlets and petitions, furiously denouncing slaveowners as criminals and sinners.

Of all the abolitionists, William Lloyd Garrison was the most forceful and sharp-tongued in his preachings. In 1831, when the antislavery movement was beginning to attract more attention,

Abolitionist William Lloyd Garrison

Garrison founded an abolitionist newspaper, *The Liberator*, in Boston. For the next thirty-five years, he tirelessly published the paper, insisting that fighting slavery was even more important than preserving the Union. Because the United States Constitution protected slavery, Garrison burned a copy of the document in public, calling it "an agreement with hell."

Naturally, the abolitionists enraged many Southerners with their fiery speeches. The planters resented these protesters for demanding freedom for slaves when *they* would never have to pay for the losses or find other ways to run the farms. The people of the South also feared that this talk would stir up their slaves. In the summer of 1831, a Virginian slave named Nat Turner led seventy black followers in a brutal revolt against the nearby community. During their bloody march from farm to farm, the slaves murdered fifty-five whites. The rebellion left Southerners terrified.

The southern states took strict measures to prevent the abolitionist movement from triggering more rebellions. They passed laws limiting the freedom of speech and the press. Abolitionist newspapers were often burned. And any stranger who arrived in town preaching against slavery was likely to be chased out by an angry mob.

Planters who once considered the possibility of freeing their slaves now vigorously defended slavery as "a positive good." They claimed that this arrangement provided slaves with food and shelter, and had rescued blacks from the "savage ways" of their African homeland. Only one in four families in the South actually owned slaves; but most whites who could not afford this luxury still sided with the wealthy planters. They too wanted to protect southern traditions, as well as their dreams of one day owning a grand plantation.

Although there were many quarrels between the North and the South, slavery became the one disagreement that was impossible to resolve. It did not matter that thousands of Northerners also disapproved of the abolitionists and scorned blacks. The freedom crusaders drowned out those other voices with their angry protests against the South. With each attack, the Southerners grew more and more resentful. Soon, even mentioning the word slavery triggered bitter disputes. ★

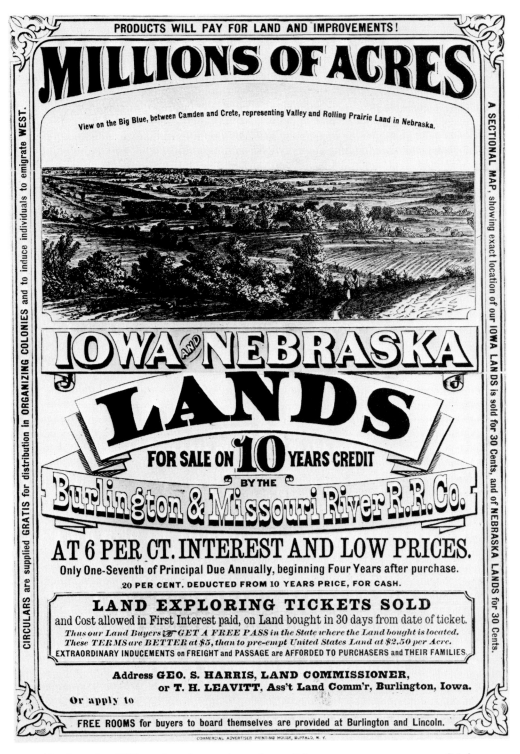

During the 1800s, advertisements such as this one were very successful in tempting ambitious foreign immigrants and Americans to buy property and settle in the wilderness of the West.

THREE

A Restless Peace

★ ★ ★ ★

In 1816 a newspaper in the rugged territory of Missouri extended a tempting invitation to the citizens of the United States. "Come on," the paper cheerfully beckoned. "We have millions of acres to occupy; provisions are cheap and in abundance."

During the 1800s, great numbers of land-hungry Americans answered the call of opportunity and set out to find their fortunes on the rich western frontier. One man who lived in St. Charles, Missouri, saw as many as a hundred pioneers pass through his town each day. Most of the settlers came from the southern states, searching for fertile new areas to plant cotton. They arrived in wagons, carriages, and carts that creaked under loads of furniture and supplies. Herds of cattle and sheep trailed behind them, driven by groups of dusty-legged slaves.

Many of the southern settlers brought their slaves to Missouri, never expecting that anyone in the West would challenge this right. The lonely frontier was far away from the parlors and meeting halls back home, where men argued over the question of slavery. But it was not long before the West was caught up in the same conflicts that haunted the North and the South.

In 1818, the Missouri Territory applied to become the twenty-third state in the Union. The settlers in the region wanted their territory to be admitted as a slave state. But leaders from the North had different ideas. James Tallmadge, a little-known politician from New York, introduced a resolution in Congress to forbid slavery in Missouri. His proposal threw Southerners into an uproar and sparked a fierce dispute among lawmakers in Washington, D.C.

Missouri was extremely important to the country's politicians. Of twenty-two states in the nation in 1818, exactly half were slave-owning and half were free. This meant there were equal numbers of senators on opposing sides, and the sections held an equal number of votes in Congress. Southern leaders cringed when they realized that Tallmadge's proposal might be accepted. If Missouri entered the nation as a free state, it would tip the balance of law-making power in favor of the North. To former president Thomas Jefferson, the debate over Missouri signaled the beginning of a long and heated struggle. Which section would gain control over the western territories, the North or the South? "The momentous question," wrote Jefferson, "like a firebell in the night, awakened and filled me with terror."

Just when Congress seemed ready to explode over the Missouri issue, a skillful peacemaker named Henry Clay stepped forward to calm the political scene. Clay, a senator from Kentucky, had a special talent for persuading men to give up their own selfish interests for the sake of the nation. Whenever he rose to deliver an address in Congress, the audience listened closely. Clay spoke in plain and simple terms, using his voice like an instrument to express emotions and ideas. As one observer commented, his voice was remarkably clear, at times "soft as a lute" and other times "full as a trumpet."

Clay became an actor during his speeches, always entertaining the audience with a showy performance. The tall and lanky speaker made spectators laugh with clever imitations of his opponents. He often gestured wildly, using his hands, his feet, his glasses, even his snuffbox, to emphasize a point. One of Clay's tricks was to crouch low and then rise to his full height of six feet as he reached the dramatic climax of his address.

With powerful speeches, Clay convinced his fellow congressmen to accept a solution to the Missouri issue that temporarily

Henry Clay, the Great Compromiser. While he became famous for steering the nation away from disunion, Clay never achieved one of his strongest political ambitions: The Kentuckian was a loser in three presidential campaigns.

satisfied both sides. Under the new agreement, Missouri would be admitted as a slave state. But to preserve the precious balance of power between the North and the South, the territory of Maine would enter the Union as a free state. The Missouri Compromise also laid down rules for the future, defining the western territories where slavery would be permitted and those where the practice would be banned.

Hoping that this solution had ended the ugly debate, many leaders in Washington began to call Henry Clay the "Great Compromiser."

Clay's Missouri Compromise kept peace in the country for almost thirty years before another crisis brought the old feuds back to life. In the spring of 1846, war broke out with Mexico. The United States declared victory two years later. As a result of the war, America gained immense new territories in the Southwest spanning nearly one million square miles. But the nation did not claim these prizes with high spirits and celebrations. Even before the Mexicans had been defeated, bickering over the future of these territories began. The first blow came from David Wilmot, a brash, tobacco-chewing congressman from Pennsylvania. Wilmot introduced a bill proposing that "neither slavery or involuntary servitude shall ever exist" in any territory that the nation might win through the Mexican War.

Wilmot's proposal sounded all too familiar—just like the resolution that had led to the Missouri conflict thirty years before. But this time the Northerners' challenge was even more threatening to the South. One southern congressman, after hearing Wilmot's measure, cried, "In the presence of the living God, if by your legislation you seek to drive us from the territories . . . I am for disunion."

Disunion. Although the frightening word had been spoken before, suddenly it sounded much more serious. In 1850, representatives from the cotton states prepared to meet in Tennessee to create a plan for dealing with the latest northern attack. Meanwhile, the Northerners held their own private strategy sessions, determined to prevent the South from introducing slavery to the new lands. It was becoming impossible to discuss matters calmly in Congress. Each formal meeting dissolved into confusion as red-faced leaders shouted taunts and insults back and forth. To many, the separation of the North and South seemed to be the only solution.

By now Henry Clay had turned seventy-three. Old age and bad health had left their scars. But even illness could not stop the famous statesman from trying once again to pull his country out of danger. On a wintry morning in 1850, Clay slowly climbed up the long flight of stairs leading to the Capitol building, stopping several times to catch his breath. When his companions suggested that he return to his hotel to rest, Clay refused. He was about to give one of the most important speeches of his life.

For weeks Clay had sat in Congress, growing more and more distressed at the hateful arguments he heard. To the spectators who watched from the balcony, Clay did not always seem to be listening very closely to the Senate meetings. They often glanced over to see the old leader concentrating on his snuffbox, or dreamily chewing a piece of striped peppermint candy. But Clay's absent-minded airs were deceiving. While his colleagues continued to quarrel, the Great Compromiser quietly began to work out a plan to save the nation from disunion.

Clay's first goal was to settle the question of slavery in the Mexican War territories without offending either side. According to his plan, California would enter the Union as a free state. In the other new lands, however, local settlers would decide whether to allow slavery or not. The plan also addressed two other nagging issues that had cropped up during the debate: the slave trade in the nation's capital and the laws governing runaway slaves. To please the Northerners, Clay recommended abolishing the sale of slaves in Washington, D.C. To make the Southerners happy, he suggested passing a strict new law called the Fugitive Slave Act, which would help slaveowners capture runaways who had escaped to the free states.

On the morning of February 5, the gallery of Congress was packed with citizens eager to hear Clay defend his great compromise. Ladies in rustling hoop skirts crowded into the red-carpeted Senate chamber. Many expected that this might be the last speech the aging leader would ever make, and they looked forward to hearing a stunning address. But as Clay rose to speak, he warned his audience that this occasion was much too serious for a showy performance. Then, in his rich voice, he made a passionate request. For the next three hours, Clay pleaded with his fellow congressmen to act with reason and relax their demands for the good of

Idealistic images such as this popular drawing gave many Americans a false impression of slavery. In this deceiving image, slaves in fresh clothing dance happily in front of their well-kept home.

the nation. One by one, he presented his resolutions, defending them with skill. In closing, Clay made one final plea: "I implore . . . that if the sad event of [disunion] shall happen, I may not survive to behold the sad and heart-rending spectacle."

Clay was exhausted but victorious when he stepped down from the speaker's platform. Many of his admirers rushed up to congratulate him with kisses and handshakes. The audience had been deeply moved by the Kentuckian's patriotic speech. After a brief vacation to recover from his illness, Clay remained in Washington long enough to see his proposals made into law. In September, Congress voted to accept the Compromise of 1850, finally ending their long debate.

With the great triumph in Washington behind him, Clay retired from Congress and returned to Lexington, Kentucky, his hometown. The citizens of Lexington welcomed him like a hero, firing cannon, ringing churchbells, and lighting bonfires in the streets. As Clay descended from his coach in front of the Phoenix Hotel, a huge crowd raised three long cheers. He stepped into the hotel and addressed the townspeople from the balcony, thanking his audience graciously and expressing his relief that the recent compromise had saved the Union. Americans now could breathe a bit more easily. Hopefully, the slavery issue was settled once and for all. As Clay looked down on the cheering crowd, he never suspected that one small measure in his compromise would actually work to ruin his country's chances for peace.

Clay had included the Fugitive Slave Act in his compromise to satisfy the South. This law promised slaveholders that the federal government would do all in its power to help recapture escaped slaves. It would send out a team of U.S. agents to supervise the arrest and return of runaways. It would even hire citizens to join in the hunt for fugitives who were harder to find.

Under the new law, runaways were no longer safe once they reached the North. Professional slave catchers roamed the streets of northern cities, searching for runaways like bloodthirsty hounds. Escaped slaves were not the only blacks to be captured. To claim the reward offered for each return, some slave hunters kidnapped blacks who had been born in the North and had lived in freedom all of their lives.

The Fugitive Slave Act was meant to tighten the South's control over slavery, but in fact it had the opposite effect. As the vicious manhunts in the streets became more common, the Northerners' hatred for slavery grew. Those who once ignored the suffering of southern blacks suddenly decided to fight back. Townspeople formed committees to rescue runaways from the patrols of slave catchers. They flocked to abolitionist meetings, plotting new ways to block the government's search for fugitives.

Northern outrage over the new act reached its peak when the slave hunters seized Anthony Burns. Burns had escaped from slavery in Virginia and found a job working in the North, in a Boston clothing store. One evening on a shadowy street, he was surrounded by six or seven men, hoisted into the air, and hauled to the courthouse where a federal marshal was waiting. Burns's former master was waiting there too, ready to take him back to Virginia.

The story of the arrest spread rapidly, and hundreds of abolitionists, both black and white, gathered for a mass meeting in a downtown hall. One angry protester after another rose to the stage and electrified the crowd with powerful speeches. "If we allow the [marshal] to take away that man," cried a young speaker, "then the word cowards should be stamped on our foreheads." The audience roared its approval, and soon the meeting was beyond control. A flood of spectators poured into the street and headed for the courthouse where Anthony Burns was being held.

Without a leader to organize them, the abolitionists turned into a violent mob. They threw stones and bricks at the windows of the courthouse. Several men pounded the door with a makeshift battering ram. When that did not work, two more rushed forward with axes and hacked out a splintery opening. But on the other side of the door, 124 guards were waiting, crouched in every hallway and along the stairs. The federal marshal had been expecting the attack. Armed with guns and sabers, his guards charged, and the riot quickly fizzled. The attempt to rescue Anthony Burns had failed.

Six days later, as Burns was led out of the courthouse, he was greeted by an amazing sight. Throngs of people lined the streets. Even the windows of the buildings were filled with people. They had come to watch him be taken away. To prevent further

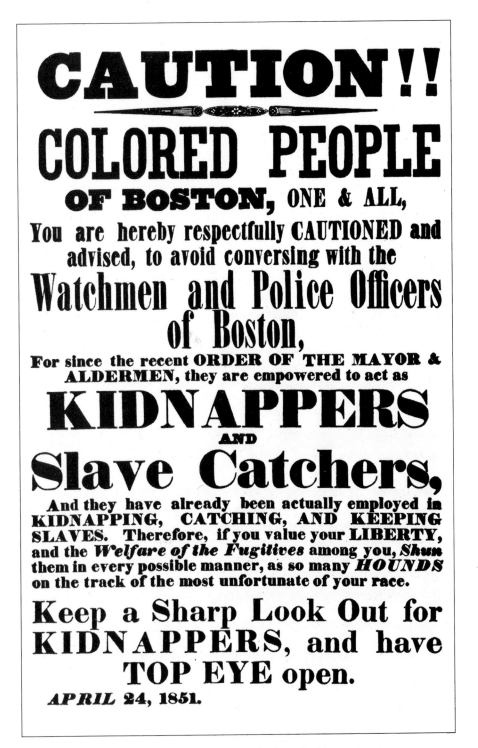

Abolitionists in Boston, Massachusetts, displayed this poster to warn runaway slaves of new dangers after the Fugitive Slave Act was passed.

Ten Dollars Reward.

RAN AWAY from the Subscriber, on the night of the 15th instant, two apprentice boys, legally bound, named WILLIAM and ANDREW JOHNSON The former is of a dark complexion, black hair, eyes, and habits. They are much of a height, about 5 feet 4 or 5 inches The latter is very fleshy, freckled face, light hair, and fair complexion. They went off with two other apprentices, advertised by Messrs Wm. & Chas. Fowler When they went away, they were well clad—blue cloth coats, light colored homespun coats, and new hats, the maker's name in the crown of the hats, is Theodore Clark. I will pay the above Reward to any person who will deliver said apprentices to me in Raleigh, or I will give the above Reward for Andrew Johnson alone

All persons are cautioned against harboring or employing said apprentices, on pain of being prosecuted.

JAMES J. SELBY, Tailor.

Raleigh, N. C. June 24, 1824   26 3t

This advertisement offered a ten-dollar reward for the return of two runaway slaves to a tailor in North Carolina. The notice also reminded the public that those caught aiding fugitives would be severely punished.

rioting, eighteen hundred armed soldiers were stationed around the courthouse square. Two hundred more tightly surrounded Burns, and the procession set out for the Boston harbor. As the troop of guards passed by, hiding their prisoner from view, a chant broke out along the street. Thousands of people began to hiss, "Shame, shame," in time with the soldiers' thudding boots. With church bells tolling, the procession continued like a funeral march, past storefronts draped in black. Finally, Anthony Burns and his captors reached the wharf, where Burns boarded a steamer back to Virginia and back to slavery.

While Burns was marched back to slavery, many other runaways found their way to freedom on the Underground Railroad. The word spread from plantation to plantation, from one slave to the next: There was a secret system called the Railroad, run by

After a cold midnight journey, weary runaways arrive at a rest station along an Underground Railroad route, where they will be sheltered and fed by sympathetic Northerners.

kind citizens who helped runaways escape to the North. Workers
on the Railroad offered fugitives food, clothing, and shelter—hide-
outs from the prowling slave catchers. They smuggled runaways in
wagons through dangerous territory and led them through woods
and alleyways to the next station along the freedom trail.

One of the most courageous workers on the Underground Railroad was a former slave named Harriet Tubman, who escaped to
freedom in 1849. When Tubman was almost thirty years old, she
slipped away from the Maryland plantation where she had toiled
as a field hand since the age of seven. She left her family behind,
resolving to return for them if she ever became free. Tubman traveled north by night, ducking into the underbrush whenever she heard
the sound of horses' hooves. For much of the journey, she waded
through swamps and streams so the slave catchers' dogs would
not be able to smell her trail.

Following the whispered directions of a white woman she had
met on the plantation, Tubman found shelter with members of the
Underground Railroad. One family kept her in their cabin for weeks,
hiding her in a potato hole until it was safe for her to continue the
journey. When Tubman finally crossed the border into the free state
of Pennsylvania, the sun was rising. "I looked at my hands to see
if I was the same person now I was free," she later said. "There
was such a glory over everything, the sun came like gold through
the trees, and over the fields, and I felt like I was in heaven."

At last Tubman had achieved her lifelong dream of freedom,
but she was not content living in Pennsylvania. She began a ten-
year quest to help free other slaves. Again and again she returned
to the South to inspire and lead more than three hundred blacks
on a dangerous escape route to the North. At one time, slave hunters
offered twelve thousand dollars for the capture of the legendary
"railroad conductor," but Tubman refused to allow any obstacles
to block her mission. She carried a pistol to ward off pursuers and
discourage frightened slaves from turning back. Tubman was once
asked if she would really shoot a runaway who threatened to turn
back. "Yes," she said. "If he was weak enough to give out, he'd
be weak enough to betray us all . . . and do you think I'd let so
many die just for one coward man?"

On one of her final and most daring expeditions, Tubman

Harriet Tubman, the legendary "conductor" of the Underground Railroad

traveled back to the plantation in Maryland to guide her parents to freedom. Disguised as an old woman, she hobbled past her former master and headed for the crude slave quarters where her parents still lived. They were too old to make the journey on foot, so Tubman stole a wagon and the threesome risked traveling on the open roads by night. With donations from members of the Underground Railroad, Tubman led her parents all the way to Canada.

Tubman ended her dangerous rescue mission in 1861, the year the Civil War began. In nineteen trips south, she had never been captured, and never lost a slave.

After serving as a spy for the Union army during the Civil War, Tubman settled with her parents in the free state of New York, where she lived until her death at the age of ninety-five.

Many white antislavery workers also took great risks to help fugitives flee to the North. Samuel Smith, a carpenter from Virginia, was caught trying to send two runaways to freedom packed in crates like loads of goods. He served an eight-year prison sentence for his so-called crimes. But despite the danger of further punishment, Smith continued his secret efforts, agreeing to help a slave named Henry Brown. Smith hid Brown in a crate that measured only three feet long and two feet wide. The box was labeled "This side up with care," and loaded on a horse-drawn cart bound for Pennsylvania. After a bumpy twenty-six hour ride, the cart finally reached Philadelphia, where several members of the Underground Railroad anxiously opened the crate. Henry "Box" Brown was safe inside. He was so overjoyed at his newfound freedom that he stepped out of the crate and promptly sang a thankful hymn.

Sympathy for runaways was spreading rapidly in the North when Harriet Beecher Stowe dealt another harsh blow to slavery in 1852. Stowe, a soft-spoken woman from New England, surprised the nation by writing *Uncle Tom's Cabin*, a daring novel that brought the evils of slavery to life. The book became an instant hit, selling three hundred thousand copies within the first year. All over the North, people read about the suffering of Stowe's characters—slaves who were sold away from their families, beaten by their masters, and hunted down by dogs. Meanwhile, southern readers clenched their fists over this new insult to their way of life. They reacted by defending the practice of slavery more stubbornly than ever.

The same year that *Uncle Tom's Cabin* was published, Henry Clay, the peacemaker, died. The spirit of compromise in the nation followed Clay to the grave. Without a leader to guide them, congressmen gave up trying to preserve peace between the North and the South. Instead, they angrily chose their sides, then waited for the next showdown over slavery to begin. ★

Harriet Beecher Stowe, author of the international bestseller *Uncle Tom's Cabin*

Disputes over slavery in Kansas led to bloody clashes between proslavery and free-soil settlers, such as the massacre on May 19, 1858, portrayed in this woodcut.

FOUR

Bloody Kansas

★ ★ ★ ★

The spring of 1856 arrived in Kansas like a long-awaited gift. Indians and traders who had lived in the territory for years could not remember a winter more severe than the last one. Life on the frontier seemed to stop during those long months, while the settlers waited for the drifting snows and freezing winds to end. Then, when the snows finally cleared, the heavy rains began.

But on the twenty-first day of May, the sun-filled air was warm and light. On the high prairies overlooking the town of Lawrence, Kansas, the ground was covered with fresh shoots of grass and tiny blue flowers shaped like bells. The hills above Lawrence were usually quiet, except for the sound of the breeze moving through the grass. But on this morning in May, the calm was broken by the arrival of hundreds of armed men.

As they reached the top of the ridge, the men looked down on the small township with wild excitement in their eyes. The long winter had made them restless. Now their chance had finally come to teach the people of Lawrence a lesson or two.

Lawrence was a gathering place for settlers who believed the spread of slavery in the territories should stop. Most abolitionist newcomers to Kansas headed for this growing town, with its fort-like buildings made of stone. Lawrence was the only free-soil settlement in Kansas—a territory ruled by pioneers who were bitterly determined to own slaves.

From the time the first building was raised in Lawrence two years before, there had been trouble between the free-soil and proslavery settlers. There were shootings, ambushes, and fires that destroyed homes. After one clash, the supporters of slavery found a way to get their revenge. A grand jury in the territory charged several leading citizens of Lawrence with treason and issued warrants for their arrest. The court added that the town's antislavery newspapers ought to be shut down and the Free State Hotel should be destroyed.

When the United States marshal heard the verdict, he publicly invited the men of Kansas to help him carry out the law. The proslavery settlers did not hesitate to respond. Like vultures, they gathered from all corners of the countryside. Many came from the bordering state of Missouri, where Southerners had won the fight for slavery several years earlier. The rugged Missouri frontiersmen, known as Border Ruffians, were a fearful sight as they rode across the Kansas plains. "I shall never forget the appearance of the lawless mob," one reporter wrote after seeing the Ruffians. ". . . Men, for the most part, of large frame, with red flannel shirts and immense boots worn outside their trousers, their faces unwashed and unshaven . . . wearing the most savage looks." They were, he added, "armed to the teeth with rifles and revolvers, cutlasses and bowie-knives."

By mid-afternoon on May 21, a posse of eight hundred men had assembled on the ridge above Lawrence. The mob was beginning to grow impatient when a messenger suddenly came riding up the hill. Shouting for attention, he announced that the "criminals" in Lawrence had surrendered quietly, and the marshal had already made his arrests. The posse, however, was not ready to be dismissed. The men surged down into the valley, led by a proslavery sheriff named Samuel Jones.

At first, the army of settlers remained orderly. They marched proudly, waving banners inscribed with "Southern Rights!" and "The Superiority of the White Race!" Several men carefully rolled cannon over the bumpy slopes. But gradually, as the posse moved closer to Lawrence and the townspeople held their fire, the pace of the march grew faster. The mob ran through the streets and soon splintered into dozens of rampaging gangs.

Sheriff Jones waved his helpers toward the two newspaper offices in town. For months, the Kansas *Free State* and the *Herald of Freedom* had enraged southern settlers with their antislavery reports. Now, Jones's men swarmed into the publishing offices, destroying whatever they could find.

"To the river!" someone yelled, and the idea quickly caught on. The men grabbed boxes of metal type used for printing, and ran to dump them in the river nearby.

When the newspaper offices lay in piles of rubble, the sheriff and his gang moved on to the Free State Hotel. After warning the owner to move his family and guests into the street, Jones ordered his gunners to fire their five cannon at the hotel. To their surprise, the heavy cannonballs barely chipped the Free State's thick stone walls. The building was constructed more like a fortress than a frontier inn. Men carried kegs of blasting powder inside and returned gleefully, their arms loaded with expensive silk drapes and bottles of liquor and wine. But the hotel still stood when the smoke from the explosives cleared. Not to be disappointed, the Ruffians set the building on fire and watched with satisfaction as it burned.

After raiding several more homes, the last gang members finally straggled out of town. The people of Lawrence came out of hiding and looked over the damage sadly. Fortunately, only one person had been killed during the assault—a proslavery man struck by a brick falling from the hotel wall. But before the next week was over, the violence would mount. It would spread from the plains of Kansas to the Senate chambers in Washington, where the decisions that caused these new uproars had been made two years before.

In 1854 Senator Stephen A. Douglas of Illinois introduced a plan to organize the territories of Kansas and Nebraska for statehood. The bill, known as the Kansas-Nebraska Act, represented the key to the senator's political dreams. To Douglas, there was nothing more important than expanding the size of the nation. He was convinced that America's strength was hidden in the West. "There is a power in the nation greater than either the North or

The citizens of Lawrence, Kansas, armed with rifles, gather to discuss the proslavery attack on their abolitionist town. In the background stand the ruins of the Free State Hotel, devastated by the mob's barrage of cannonballs, explosives, and fire.

the South," Douglas declared in a Senate speech, "a growing, increasing, swelling power, that will be able to speak the law to this nation. . . . That power is the country known as the Great West."

However, Douglas knew that the admission of more western states to the Union would remain stalled as long as the issue of slavery stood in the way. Under the Missouri Compromise of 1820, slavery had been outlawed in Kansas and Nebraska. Because of this rule, southern senators wanted to prevent any attempts to organize these territories into states. One congressman announced that

Senator Stephen Douglas of Illinois, author of the Kansas-Nebraska Act. A hard-driving politician, Douglas was fiercely determined to open the West for expansion.

he would see Nebraska "sink in hell" before voting to admit the territory as a free state.

With the Kansas-Nebraska Act, Douglas found a way to win the support of southern leaders and move ahead with his plans to develop an empire in the West. His new bill boldly rejected the Missouri Compromise, stating that the question of slavery in the territories should be decided by the people who settled there. The settlers themselves, not congressmen, should vote on whether Kansas and Nebraska should enter the Union as free or slave states.

While Douglas expected his policy to cause a stir in Congress, he was not prepared for the strength of the reaction. For Northerners, the Kansas-Nebraska Act was the very last straw. Tempers exploded in the debates that followed. During one hectic meeting at the Capitol, the sergeant-at-arms was ordered to arrest a congressman who raised a weapon against another.

Stephen Douglas was not to be daunted by protests from the North. He fought for the Kansas-Nebraska Act with all the determination of a charging bull. Although the senator stood only five feet four inches tall, he made others forget his small stature with his aggressive style. Nicknamed the "Little Giant," he addressed Congress in a booming voice, forcefully arguing the merits of his bill. During Senate recesses, he sought out his doubters one-by-one and bargained smoothly for their votes.

Despite its many opponents, the Kansas-Nebraska Act was approved by Congress. President Franklin Pierce signed the famous bill in May of 1854, making it into law. But as soon as the battle in Congress was over, another more brutal contest in Kansas began. The South desperately wanted to reserve Kansas for slavery; the North was just as determined to declare the territory free. Under the new law, the side that arrived there first with the most settlers would win.

The race for Kansas seemed to begin the moment the president signed the bill and set down his pen. In Massachusetts, a society was formed to encourage antislavery citizens to head for the plains. The organization published a pamphlet, stating that it would raise five million dollars to assist thousands of free-soil settlers in making the journey to Kansas. Proslavery groups formed their own companies, hoping to attract a large number of South-

Lured by promises of fertile land and a chance to help decide the territory's future, hundreds of adventurous people joined the rush to settle in Kansas.

erners to the territory. The Missouri Emigrant Company wrote to newspapers in the South: "We tell you that unless you come quickly and by the thousands, we are gone . . . then farewell to the Southern Cause, and farewell to our glorious Union."

As the months passed, the pleas for settlers became more and more urgent. The date for an election in Kansas had been announced. In March of 1855, the settlers would vote to elect members of a territorial board, which would create laws and officially decide on the future of slavery in Kansas. When news of the upcoming election spread, the Border Ruffians from Missouri went into action. They traveled across the border to pose as settlers from Kansas and cast illegal votes for proslavery candidates. Hoping to win the nearby territory for slavery, even the leaders of Missouri urged citizens from their state to break the voting laws. "When you reside within one day's journey of the territory," proclaimed

Heavily armed and eager for a brawl, the Border Ruffians invaded Kansas
to cast illegal votes for slavery.

one senator, "you can, without an exertion, send five hundred of your young men who will vote in favor of your institutions."

The Border Ruffians' strategy worked just as they had planned. When the ballots were counted, they showed that thirty-six proslavery lawmakers had been elected, and only three free-soil men. "All Hail! Proslavery Party Victorious!" cried a Missouri newspaper. " . . . Bring your slaves and fill up the Territory. Kansas is saved." As the new legislature set to work, the abolitionists' worst fears quickly came true. First, the proslavery members of the board forced the free-soilers to resign. Then they passed a list of severe laws designed to protect slavery. According to the new rules, those who helped fugitives to escape would be hanged; even mentioning misgivings about slavery could lead to jail.

In a rage, the free-soilers decided to defy the legislature and set up their own government. They elected a new lawmaking council and governor, pronounced slavery illegal in Kansas, and applied to Washington to make their territory a free state. Knowing this would infuriate the local Southerners, the antislavery settlers hurriedly began to prepare for a fight. They armed themselves with rifles sent from New England. In the streets of Lawrence, men practiced marching and military drills.

Throughout the autumn of 1855, free-soil and proslavery settlers clashed again and again. By the following spring, hatred and confusion had spread across the plains of Kansas like a terrible disease.

In Washington, feelings over the slavery issue in the West were growing just as strained. On May 20, 1856, the day before Lawrence was raided, Senator Charles Sumner of Massachusetts ended a stinging, two-day speech against the slavery movement in Kansas. In his address, Sumner sharply criticized several of his opponents. The main target of his attack was Andrew Butler, an aging proslavery senator from South Carolina who happened to be away from Congress at the time. Sumner accused Butler of twisting the truth and made fun of the old gentleman's speeches and conversation. "He cannot [open] his mouth, but out there flies a blunder," said Sumner. His remarks offended many members of Congress, angering the Southerners and even several of Sumner's abolitionist friends.

Soon, people throughout the country were discussing the "Crime Against Kansas" address—but not for the reasons Sumner had planned. Two days after his speech, Sumner sat writing letters in the nearly empty Senate chamber, with his legs stretched out under his desk. Suddenly, he noticed that someone was standing beside him—a man he did not recognize.

"I have read your speech twice over, carefully," said the

Senator Charles Sumner of Massachusetts. Angered by the events in the territories, the antislavery leader prepared a two-day Senate speech called "The Crime Against Kansas." As he told a friend a few days before the address, "My soul is wrung by this outrage, and I shall pour it forth."

stranger. "It is a libel on South Carolina and Mr. Butler, who is a relative of mine . . ." Without finishing his sentence, the man raised his cane high into the air and swung it down on Senator Sumner's head.

The attacker was Preston Brooks, a young congressman from South Carolina and a distant cousin of Andrew Butler. For two days he had lingered about the Capitol, waiting for a chance to defend the honor of his cousin and his state. Now, with powerful blows, he struck Sumner again and again. Stunned by the assault,

In this newspaper illustration depicting the caning of Senator Charles Sumner, the artist also invented an interesting sideline scene. While several congressmen in the background watch the beating in distress, others laugh and try to prevent Sumner's friends from coming to his aid.

the senator struggled to rise, wrenching his desk loose from its bolts in the floor. He lurched to his feet, but Congressman Brooks still swung at him with his gold-headed cane, even when it began to splinter into smaller and smaller pieces.

Finally, several other congressmen came running to stop the attack. One senator caught Sumner as he sank to the floor covered with blood. Brooks then strolled away, tossing his black hair and straightening his coat. He later described his deed proudly: "I . . . gave him about thirty first rate stripes. . . . Every lick went where I intended. For about the first five or six licks he offered to make fight. . . . Towards the last he bellowed like a calf."

More than three years passed before Sumner recovered enough from his injuries to return to Congress. Meanwhile, his empty desk in the Senate chamber served as a constant reminder of the vicious beating and the nation's dispute over slavery. Northerners were outraged by the assault on Sumner, and the Southerners' reaction to the incident angered them even more than the caning itself. Preston Brooks became a hero in the South. Instead of arresting Brooks for his crime, the courts merely charged the congressman a fine of three hundred dollars. From all over the South came letters of praise for Brooks and gifts of fancy canes. One cane was engraved with the message, "Hit Him Again."

When news of Sumner's beating reached Kansas, one man was ready to strike back with dangerous force. John Brown, a devout abolitionist, had just heard of the attack on Lawrence the day before. Now, this story from Washington stretched his patience to the snapping point. As one of his sons reported, Brown "went crazy—*crazy*" when he heard the news. "It seemed to be the finishing, decisive touch." After that moment, nothing could stop Brown from carrying out his plans.

For John Brown, fighting slavery had been a lifelong mission. He had struggled for years to become a successful businessman, failing at each occupation he tried. By the age of fifty-six, "Old Man" Brown had watched fifteen of his business ventures end in disaster. But as he wandered from state to state looking for new ways to support his large family, Brown never gave up his war against slavery. In Ohio he kept a shelter for runaways on the Underground Railroad. In New York he formed a society that

John "Old Man" Brown, the leader of the Pottawatomie Massacre. This photograph, which Brown's family regarded as his "best picture," captures the antislavery crusader's rigid personality in his grim expression and piercing stare.

encouraged blacks to band together and use weapons to oppose the Fugitive Slave Law. And when Brown learned of the slavery crisis in Kansas, he loaded his one-horse wagon with guns and swords and moved west.

In Kansas, Brown organized a small company of abolitionists, including four of his sons. Two of the sons, Oliver and Frederick, disapproved of their father's brutal scheme to take revenge for the attacks on Lawrence and Sumner. Yet John Brown had a special talent for persuading men to carry out his wishes. With irresistible energy, the old man convinced his followers that they were acting out the will of God. As he spoke of slavery, his lean face hardened and his eyes shone with a fierce light. It was time to "fight fire with fire," he shouted, to "strike terror in the hearts of the proslavery people." Before long, each of Brown's men had fallen under his overpowering spell.

It was nearly midnight on May 24, 1856, when John Brown and his companions reached the first stop on their deadly expedition. They had come to the cabin of Henry Doyle, a well-known proslavery man in the settlement near Pottawatomie Creek. Brown banged loudly on the door and asked for directions to a neighbor's house. Fooled by the voice, Doyle opened the door, only to be thrown back as the armed strangers burst into the cabin and announced that the northern army had come to call. As Mrs. Doyle begged for her family's life, the old man ordered Doyle and his two oldest boys to step outside.

Out in the darkness, Brown's men flew at the Doyles with broadswords. After a moment of flashing blades, their work was done. The killers then moved on, leaving their three victims lying dead along the prairie road. They did not wash their swords until they had murdered two more proslavery men. It made no difference that these settlers were not involved with the march on Lawrence. John Brown was obsessed with destroying slavery and its supporters.

The massacre at Pottawatomie marked the end of a week of violence across the nation. After only seven days, a town lay in ruin, Congress was in turmoil, and several settlers were dead. In the fall of 1856, a new governor, appointed by the federal government, arrived in Kansas. With his bold manner and six-foot, five-inch frame, John Geary was a powerful figure in the territory. He reigned over the proslavery and free-soil settlers with the same hardfisted rules. With the backing of U.S. Army troops, Geary quickly brought order to Kansas. But as the governor soon learned, peace could not last—in Kansas or across the nation. The bloody week in May had been merely a preview of events to come. ★

Abraham Lincoln as a presidential candidate in 1860. Shortly after this photograph was taken, Lincoln received a letter from an eleven-year-old girl
urging him to wear whiskers because his face was too thin. He promptly
grew a thick beard, which gave him the distinguished appearance that most
people remember today.

FIVE

A Man Named Lincoln

★ ★ ★ ★

On August 21, 1858, twelve thousand people flocked to the dusty town square of Ottawa, Illinois, and waited impatiently for the great showdown to begin. They had come from miles around to watch a heated debate between the two challengers competing for the office of senator in Illinois. The more famous candidate was Stephen Douglas, the fireball congressman who had created such a ruckus by introducing the Kansas-Nebraska Act in 1854. His opponent was a plainspoken country lawyer named Abraham Lincoln. The two men were longtime political rivals. They had stood on opposite sides of national issues ever since their first meeting twenty-five years before.

Throughout the 1800s, political speeches were a favorite form of entertainment for Americans. The debate between Lincoln and Douglas was the social event of the season in Ottawa. As more and more people arrived and streamed toward the wooden plat-form in the center of town, the gathering took on a carnival air. Bands and military companies paraded through the dirt streets beneath a canopy of bright banners and flags. On each corner peddlers cried out, tempting the crowds to buy their wares. At the public square a group of spectators, eager for the debate to begin, climbed on the wooden awning above the stage. Suddenly, the overhang gave way, dumping its load of men and boys on the heads of the reception committee below.

At last the two candidates appeared. They had arrived in town in very different styles. Lincoln rode into Ottawa on a crowded train filled with his supporters, while Douglas came in an elegant carriage drawn by four purebred horses. Four miles outside of the town, the Little Giant was met by hundreds of his admirers, who escorted him to his hotel amid the booming of cannon. Once the candidates had pushed their way to the platform, it took officials a half hour to bring the excited crowd to order. At two-thirty Douglas rose and opened the debate. For the next three hours, the competitors battled with words under the scorching August sun.

Just as the audience had expected, Douglas immediately tackled the subject of slavery. On this issue, like most, the candidates strongly disagreed. Abraham Lincoln was a member of the Republican party, a political group founded to halt the spread of slavery through government action. Douglas, a member of the rival Democratic party, had once revealed that he did not care whether slavery "was voted down or voted up." He believed that each state should have the right to decide this question for itself.

Another recent event had driven the candidates even further apart in their views. In 1857 the U.S. Supreme Court reached a decision in the case of a slave named Dred Scott. The verdict stunned antislavery forces across the nation. Dred Scott had been the personal servant of Dr. John Emerson, an army surgeon. When Emerson was transferred to posts in Illinois and the Wisconsin Territory, he brought Scott along. Four years later the surgeon's assignments in these free lands were complete, and he carried his servant back to the slave state of Missouri. When his master died, Scott decided to sue the courts for his liberty, arguing that the years he had spent on free soil made him a free man.

For more than ten years the case dragged through the courts, raising many prickly questions along the way. As a black man, did Scott have the right to sue in the federal courts? Was a slaveowner entitled to take his servants into the free territories of the United States?

When the eighty-year-old chief justice, Roger Taney, announced the Supreme Court's decision, the ruling was startling in its strictness. Scott did not have the right to sue, the judge declared in a high, thin voice. Blacks, even if they were free, were not citizens. Therefore, Taney continued, they were not entitled to the same privileges as whites. As for Scott's freedom, this was also denied. Taney stated that slaves were property, and owners certainly had the right to take their property onto free soil. And carrying the ruling one step further, the chief justice proclaimed that Congress had no power to keep slavery out of the territories.

While opponents of slavery were dismayed by the Dred Scott decision, Douglas and most Democrats completely agreed with Taney's opinion about the inferiority of blacks. As the huge crowd in Ottawa, Illinois, listened closely, Douglas boasted these views with a thundering voice and clenched fists. "For one, I am opposed to Negro citizenship in any and every form," Douglas cried. "I believe this government was made on the white basis. I believe it was made by white men, for the benefit of white men."

As he talked about slavery, Douglas tested the strategy that he would rely on throughout his campaign. Douglas knew that many of the whites who opposed slavery were also prejudiced toward blacks. In speech after speech, he shrewdly played upon the voters' racial fears. "Are you in favor of [giving] the Negro the rights and privileges of citizenship?" Douglas asked the crowd. Are you for letting Negroes flow into Illinois and "cover your prairies with black settlements?" "No! No!" someone answered. Do you want Negroes to vote and marry with white people? "Never!" yelled several whites. If you're for all this, Douglas bellowed, "then support Mr. Lincoln and the Black Republican party."

Cheered on by his supporters, Douglas hotly defended his policy of allowing the people to decide on the question of slavery. He insisted that the Founding Fathers had made America a divided land—half slave and half free—for good reasons. "They knew that the laws and regulations which would suit the granite hills of New Hampshire would be unsuited to the rice plantations of South Carolina," Douglas said. Peace could not exist in the nation unless each state had "the full and complete power to do as it pleased." Douglas accused Lincoln of steering the nation toward civil war by trying to wipe out slavery across the land. "I believe that this

In this illustration of the "Great Debates," Lincoln delivers his antislavery message to an attentive audience while Stephen Douglas waits his turn to reply.

new doctrine preached by Mr. Lincoln and his party will dissolve the Union if it succeeds."

Rising to reply, Lincoln looked like a poor match for the Little Giant's high-handed ways. Douglas was dressed in the style of a wealthy plantation owner, wearing a wide-brimmed white hat, a ruffled shirt, and a dark blue coat with shining buttons. Next to the stocky congressman, Lincoln—standing six feet, four inches— appeared gangly and awkward in his ill-fitting suit. When he began to address the crowd, his voice sounded sharp and a key too high.

But despite his humble ways, Lincoln commanded a large

number of supporters in the audience. Republican forces and anti-slavery feelings were strong in the free state of Illinois—especially in the northern part of the state, where Ottawa was located. The audience applauded so wildly for Lincoln when he rose to speak that he had to wait several minutes before he could be heard. Once the spectators had calmed down to listen, they were charmed by Lincoln's wit and the sincere look in his deep-set eyes. They interrupted the speaker again and again with cheers and shouts of encouragement.

In his speech, Lincoln set out to deny Douglas's charges one by one. He claimed that the senator was twisting and misrepresenting his views, using "a fantastic arrangement of words, by which a man can prove a horse chestnut to be a chestnut horse." First, Lincoln explained, he had never said that blacks should be given perfect equality with whites, as his opponent had claimed. "But," he added, "there is no reason in the world why the Negro is not entitled to all the natural rights enumerated in the Declaration of Independence, the right to life, liberty and the pursuit of happiness."

As for the suggestion that he wanted to sweep out slavery with one stroke, Lincoln insisted that this charge was also untrue. He had no intention of interfering with slavery in the states where it already existed. His goal was to stop the spread of slavery in the territories. Once this was accomplished, the practice in other areas would gradually die out on its own. Otherwise, Lincoln warned, Democrats like Douglas would push slavery forward until it was "lawful in all the states, old as well as new, North as well as South."

The sun was beginning to set when Lincoln and Douglas stepped down from the stage, but the battle between the candidates was not over. The two rivals met in six other towns across the state for a series of outdoor debates. At each stop, thousands of people dropped their chores for the day and pushed through the dust-choked streets to hear the candidates and choose their favorite man. Soon people throughout the nation were eager for news of the exciting Senate race in Illinois. Everywhere the Little Giant and "Long Abe" went, a flock of reporters trailed close behind.

After four exhausting months of speechmaking, it was time

for the candidates to return home and wait for the voters to cast their ballots. Lincoln was anxiously pacing the telegraph office in Springfield, Illinois, when the results came in. Douglas had won the election by a narrow margin of votes. The defeat cast a gloomy shadow over Lincoln. It was not easy to shrug off all the weary hours of campaigning or his supporters' disappointed faces. "I feel like the boy who stumped his toe," Lincoln told his friends. "I am too big to cry and too badly hurt to laugh."

Yet the Senate campaign had not been a complete loss. The "Great Debates" had thrown Lincoln into the spotlight, and created a national reputation for this prairie lawyer and his noble ideas. A few Republican newspapers in Illinois were even hinting that Lincoln would make a fine candidate for president. While Lincoln did not take these reports seriously, many others did—including his friend Jesse Fell, a leading Republican in Illinois.

One December evening, shortly after the Senate election, Fell met Lincoln coming out of the courthouse in the town of Bloomington. He caught his friend by the arm and led him to a nearby law office to discuss his latest notion. Fell had just returned from a trip to the eastern states. Everywhere Republicans had talked about Douglas's tough opponent, and asked, "Who is this man Lincoln?" If the nation learned more about his background and antislavery efforts, Fell told Lincoln excitedly, he could become a serious challenger for the presidency.

When Fell had finished outlining his plan, Lincoln still was not convinced. "I admit that I am ambitious and would like to be president," he replied. "But there is no such good luck in store for me . . . besides there is nothing in my early history that would interest you or anybody else." With those words, Lincoln wrapped an old gray shawl around his bony shoulders, said good night, and stepped off into the cold night.

Once again Lincoln turned his attention to his law practice in Springfield, but he still remained active in the Republican party. Gradually he discovered that he had been wrong about the public's interest in his personal life. People were fascinated by tales of his humble childhood on the frontier—how he lived in a log cabin, earned money by splitting fence rails, and worked his way up from a backwoods farm boy to a respected young lawyer. Even more important, political figures and citizens from all over the country were anxious to hear his views on slavery and the future of the nation. Republican groups from Kansas to New York invited Lincoln to come and speak. As the election of 1860 drew closer, running for the office of president no longer seemed like such a farfetched idea.

In the fall of 1859, Lincoln began to address a new subject in his speeches: John Brown and his crusade for freedom. The massacre of five proslavery men in Kansas had not been enough for this obsessed abolitionist and his followers. When the uproar over his crime had quieted in the West, Brown moved on to the rocky hills of Maryland. There he spent the summer in a rented farmhouse, filling his hideout with weapons and putting the final touches on his master plan.

For years Brown had dreamed of leading a rebellion of slaves. He was convinced that blacks all over the South were burning with hatred for their white masters and were on the verge of a huge revolt. As Brown lay awake at nights plotting this uprising, his schemes became more and more grand. He would personally lead the daring march through the thickly wooded mountains of Maryland and Virginia. At the town of Harpers Ferry, where the two states touched borders, he and a trusted band of followers would capture the federal weapons supply house. When the time came, hundreds of slaves would break away from the plantations and swarm to his side. Together, he and his army would transform the South into a land of freedom.

Brown was so dazzled by his ambitious ideas that he ignored the practical details essential for success. He never carefully explored Harpers Ferry to find secret trails and hiding places for escape. He never worked out emergency plans in case his attack went wrong. And most surprising, Brown did not even bother to warn all the slaves in the area that the rebellion was about to take place. The Old Man believed the invasion would go smoothly because God would "guard and shield" him and show his army the path to safety.

On October 18, 1859, thirty-six hours after his raiders stormed the weapons arsenal in Harpers Ferry, Brown finally realized that his mission was doomed. Instead of inspiring a mighty uprising, his dreams had ended in horrible failure. When news of the attack spread to nearby farms, not a single slave rushed to join the rebellion. Without organization and a leader to guide them, many slaves were unprepared for this bold move. Others were too frightened of the punishment they would suffer if captured. So Brown, trapped in the arsenal at Harpers Ferry, faced hundreds of armed and furious townspeople with only twenty-one men at his side.

Rumors of Brown's attack swept through the South like shock waves. After seizing the armory, the raiders took prisoners during the drizzly night, and fatally wounded a railroad worker who stumbled onto the scene. By morning churches in towns through-

John Brown's raid threw the ordinarily peaceful town of Harpers Ferry into chaos and brought the riverfront community instant fame.

out Virginia and Maryland were tolling bells of alarm. The tele-graph wires sent out exaggerated accounts of the attack: "Negro Rebellion at Harpers Ferry!" "Slaves Rampaging and Murdering in the Streets!" When they heard the reports, southern whites reacted hysterically. The nightmare that had frightened them for years was coming true. Farmers from the surrounding countryside grabbed their shotguns, axes, or any weapon they could find, and headed for Harpers Ferry. With special orders from Washington to protect the citizens from attack, ninety U.S. Marines boarded a train for the little mountain town.

The townsmen showed no mercy for John Brown and his followers. They pumped bullets into the fire-engine house and rifle works where most of the raiders had retreated in confusion. When Brown sent his son Watson and another messenger out under a white flag of truce, the mob in the streets gunned both men down. At the sight of the vicious crowd outside, the youngest of the raid-ers lost his courage and tried to escape. But as he dashed across the railroad tracks and jumped into the Potomac River, he was chased down by a group of citizens and shot to death at close range.

Inside the engine house, John Brown paced back and forth in the shadows, trying to decide what to do next. His scattered raid-ers had killed the mayor of Harpers Ferry and a slaveowner. News of the latest deaths, along with whiskey from the local tavern, made the townspeople and militiamen more violent. But as always, Brown remained unshakable, his eyes still blazing with a stubborn light. His two wounded sons lay in the corner of the building, both of them crying out in pain. One of Brown's prisoners later recalled that Oliver Brown begged his father to shoot him and end his agony. The Old Man turned to his son and answered bitterly, "If you must die, die like a man."

It was not until the next morning, after he peered out into the courtyard, that Brown admitted the rebellion was over. The com-pany of marines had arrived. Now they stood ready to charge the engine house, armed with bayonets and sledgehammers.

The two thousand spectators who had gathered in the streets cheered as the soldiers stormed the building, and they eagerly waited for the villains to be marched out to face punishment. Many of the townspeople were surprised by what they saw. No army of abolitionists appeared from the engine house. The leader of the revolt was an old man, unconscious and bleeding, with a flowing white beard. There were only four other raiders left to stand trial. Ten of Brown's followers had been killed, and the rest had escaped into the mountains.

Although no slave war ever took place, the incident at Harpers Ferry sent a tidal wave of panic across the South, just as Brown had hoped. For weeks after the raid, whites lived in fear that their slaves would turn against them at any moment. If a barn accidentally burned down or a slave escaped, rumors of a revolt sprung up like weeds. To aggravate matters, hundreds of Northerners were calling John Brown a champion of freedom—"the bravest and

Suffering from injuries from the raid on Harpers Ferry, John Brown spent his trial lying on a bed in the courtroom. But he insisted on standing to argue his own case.

humanest man in all the country." Southerners were deeply offended by this praise. Many insisted that the attack was just another step in the Yankees' plot to eliminate slavery and bring down the South. They pointed fingers at Republicans in particular, claiming that the party's abolitionist speeches had inspired Brown's bloody act.

John Brown was hanged for his crime in December of 1859, but his restless spirit continued to haunt the nation. In the South a warlike mood filled the air. Thousands of men joined military companies, eagerly preparing for the day when "those Black Republicans" would decide to strike again. State lawmakers devoted more public money to the purchase of weapons. Visitors from the North found that they were no longer welcome in southern cities and towns.

As the election year of 1860 opened, Abraham Lincoln tried to break through this atmosphere of hostility and distrust. "Let us Republicans do our part" to preserve peace and harmony throughout the country, he told his fellow party members. "Even though much provoked, let us do nothing through passion and ill temper. Even though the southern people will not so much as listen to us, let us calmly consider their demands." There were several well-known Republicans competing for the presidency in 1860. While Lincoln was not the favorite choice for many voters, this peace-making approach won him a great deal of support.

In May the Republican party held its national convention in Chicago, Illinois, to choose a presidential candidate. By the opening day of the meeting, the city was overflowing with enthusiastic convention-goers. Republican representatives from all over the Union had traveled to Chicago to cast their ballots. Every hotel was packed with delegates, reporters, and ordinary citizens swept along by the excitement of the affair. The crowd for the convention was so large that the Republicans of Chicago built a special hall for the event— a gigantic barnlike building nicknamed the Wigwam.

Although Lincoln was not expected to win the nomination, his followers outnumbered other supporters at the convention. With only a short distance to travel, citizens from around Illinois poured into Chicago to cheer for Honest Abe. To help Lincoln's campaign along, one group of young men printed stacks of counterfeit convention tickets to hand out to his supporters. When the doors of the Wigwam opened, Lincoln men shoved into the drafty galleries, crowding out the opponents' followers.

From the moment the convention was called to order, Lincoln's campaign managers worked feverishly to promote their candidate. As they busily moved among the delegates in the convention hall and hotel lobbies, they made a special effort to point out the drawbacks of the other candidates. One had owned slaves in the past, which contradicted the principles of many Republicans. Another was widely considered to be too extreme and dangerous in his views. Clearly, Lincoln was the candidate of compromise—the only challenger who could satisfy all sides of the party at once.

On the third day of the convention, the commotion inside the Wigwam shook the rough wooden floorboards. It was time for the nominating to begin. The chairman of the convention called the roll, and representatives from each state and territory rose to announce how their delegates had voted. During the first round of balloting, Lincoln's strongest rival, William Seward of New York, led the race. But slowly, the number of votes for Lincoln began to climb. His supporters screamed with the growing suspense and threw their black hats into the air. One reporter, hoping to give his readers some idea of the deafening noise, wrote: "Imagine all the hogs ever slaughtered in Cincinnati giving their death squeals together, a score of big steam whistles going. . . . A herd of buffalos or lions could not have made a more tremendous roaring."

At last the final votes were announced. As the clerks tallied the ballots, the crowd of ten thousand fell silent. Campaign managers hushed their hoarse chattering; ladies stopped fluttering their fans. Suddenly, the leader of the Ohio delegation leaped onto his chair and announced the change of four more votes to Lincoln. The spectators broke into a roar of approval, and the tension of the past three days faded from the hall. Lincoln, the backwoods rail splitter, had captured the Republican presidential nomination.

By now Lincoln's chances for the presidency were beginning to look strong. Two weeks earlier the national Democratic convention had met in Charleston, South Carolina, and the meeting had ended in disaster. Unlike the Republicans, the Democrats could not agree on the issue of slavery. Delegates from the South wanted to adopt federal laws that would protect the rights of slaveholders anywhere in the Union; delegates from the North wanted to allow the people of each state to decide on the problem. When the Northerners refused to surrender to their demands, fifty southern Democrats stormed out of the Charleston convention, vowing that they would never support the Yankees' choice for president.

Efforts to reunite the group were hopeless, and the party divided into two separate wings. The northern Democrats met in Baltimore, Maryland, and nominated Lincoln's old rival, Stephen Douglas, for president. Southern Democrats quickly organized their own convention in Richmond, Virginia, and nominated John C. Breckinridge of Kentucky. Republicans were delighted with news

In this Republican campaign poster, Lincoln is pictured with his vice presidential running mate, Hannibal Hamlin. As the rustic figures at the bottom of the poster show, Lincoln represented more than freedom to his supporters; he was also a symbol of the pioneering spirit, hard work, and the great frontier.

of the split. The more the Democratic party stumbled, the more powerful the Republicans became.

On election day, November 6, 1860, Lincoln remained remarkably calm. Even when the returns began to show a Republican lead, and his friends whooped with pleasure, Lincoln sat sprawled on the couch in the Springfield telegraph office. He listened quietly as the instrument clicked out its messages and the operator happily announced the results: Citizens from Illinois had voted Republican; the same was true in California, Pennsylvania, and the crucial state of New York. Lincoln had swept the northern states.

Around midnight, the results from the southern states began to appear, telling a different story. "Now, we shall get a few licks back," Lincoln commented from his place on the sofa. Many southern states had not even placed his name on their ballots. Yet the number of northern votes was large enough to keep Lincoln ahead in the race. With the telegraph lines still humming, he and his friends left for a banquet given by the Republican ladies of Springfield. The hostesses greeted Lincoln with a new air of respect. They clustered around him, offering him sandwiches and coffee. Admirers serenaded him with Republican songs. But Lincoln was too restless to enjoy this special treatment. He soon returned to the telegraph office and watched over the results until his election was certain.

Although Lincoln did not go to bed until long after midnight, he could not sleep. Outside, triumphant Republicans were parading through the streets. The windowpanes rattled with the blast of a victory cannon. But Lincoln barely heard these sounds of celebration. As he lay awake, his enormous new responsibilities preoccupied his thoughts. He would soon become president of a nation that was deeply divided. Could he find a way to settle the old arguments once and for all? Could he break down the barriers between the North and the South?

The task would be more difficult than Lincoln ever imagined. In the days before the election, many Southerners had warned that a "Black Republican" victory would surely mean disunion. "Let the consequences be what they may . . . the South will never submit to such humiliation and degradation as the inauguration of Abraham Lincoln," a newspaper in Georgia proclaimed. Yet southern

Standing in front of the unfinished U.S. Capitol on March 4, 1861, Lincoln delivers the first address of his presidency to an audience of thirty thousand. Armed troops were stationed throughout the crowd to guard against southern attempts to harm the president or disrupt his speech.

Roused by speechmakers on the balcony of a Charleston hotel, southern patriots cheer for secession and independence.

leaders had been threatening to withdraw from the Union for years. Most Republicans, including Lincoln, believed this talk of secession was nothing more than bluff and exaggeration.

In December of 1860, South Carolina proved the doubting Republicans wrong. Delegates from across the state met in Charleston and voted unanimously to establish an independent nation—one where the right to own slaves would never be questioned. The years of southern indecision came to an end. Soon seven other southern states rushed to leave the Union. Americans everywhere turned their attention toward Charleston, the hotbed of the rebellion, and a huge brick fort within the city's harbor. ★

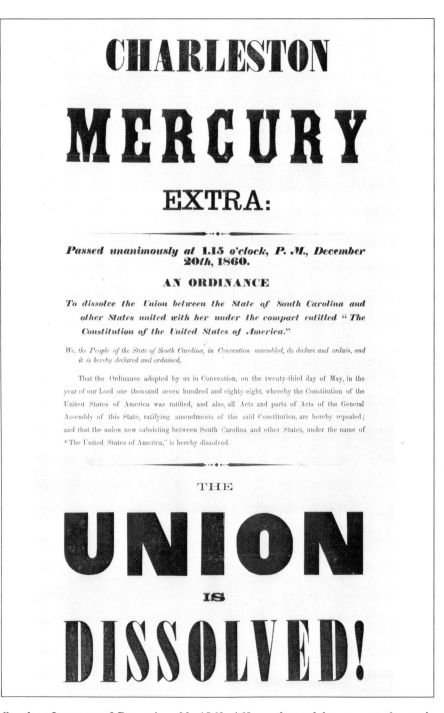

CHARLESTON
MERCURY
EXTRA:

Passed unanimously at 1.15 o'clock, P. M., December 20th, 1860.

AN ORDINANCE

To dissolve the Union between the State of South Carolina and other States united with her under the compact entitled " The Constitution of the United States of America."

We, the People of the State of South Carolina, in Convention assembled, do declare and ordain, and it is hereby declared and ordained,

That the Ordinance adopted by us in Convention, on the twenty-third day of May, in the year of our Lord one thousand seven hundred and eighty-eight, whereby the Constitution of the United States of America was ratified, and also, all Acts and parts of Acts of the General Assembly of this State, ratifying amendments of the said Constitution, are hereby repealed ; and that the union now subsisting between South Carolina and other States, under the name of "The United States of America," is hereby dissolved.

THE
UNION
IS
DISSOLVED!

On the afternoon of December 20, 1860, 169 southern delegates voted unanimously to cut the ties between South Carolina and the United States. Fifteen minutes after the vote was passed, this special edition of a Charleston newspaper rolled off the presses.

Many southern women wept as they watched the first battle of the Civil War from the rooftops of Charleston.

SIX

The Guns Roar

★　★　★　★

Just before dawn on April 12, 1861, Mary Chesnut braced herself for the roar of the first shot on Fort Sumter. She thought of her husband, a colonel in the Confederate Army, who waited somewhere in the dark and dangerous harbor. As the bells in St. Michael's church chimed four o'clock, the shot still did not come. Mrs. Chesnut began to hope for a miracle. Perhaps the Confederate and federal forces had worked out a compromise. But nothing could stop the conflict that had been building for a half century or more. At four-thirty the heavy booming of a cannon shook Mrs. Chesnut's hotel room, and she ran to join the other guests who had gathered on the rooftop to watch the Confederate shells bursting over the harbor.

All over Charleston southern citizens rushed to their rooftops or the waterfront to witness the dramatic scene. They watched the battle with mixed emotions. "Who could tell what each volley accomplished of death and destruction," Mary Chesnut wrote in her diary. "The women were wild, there on the housetop." Fearing for the safety of their husbands and sons who were fighting in the harbor, many of the women wept or prayed. The men on the shore cheered on the Confederates and yelled curses at the Yankees as if the soldiers in the distant forts could hear every word. Exhausted from all the excitement, Mrs. Chesnut sank down on what she thought was a black stool. "Get up, you foolish woman—your dress is on fire," a man cried as he ran forward to put out the sparks in her clothes. Mrs. Chesnut had sat on a hot chimney.

As daybreak approached and the sounds of Confederate cannon fire rumbled on, the guns at Fort Sumter remained strangely quiet. Major Anderson was in no hurry to enter the battle. For

Dressed in new uniforms and bearing a new flag, Confederate soldiers at Charleston stand jauntily at attention. The seven stars in the flag represent the southern states that had left the Union by the time the first shot was fired at Fort Sumter.

months he had tried to prevent this dreadful ordeal. To add to his distress, the promised relief ships loaded with more weapons and food still had not arrived. With shells crashing into the parade ground above them, the Union soldiers huddled in a bombproof shelter for another grim breakfast of salt pork and water. When the officers had finished their meal, Anderson assembled his men for final instructions. Lined up with the soldiers were eight musicians and forty-eight workmen, who had been stranded in the fort when the conflict began. In the face of an enemy many times its size, the tiny army needed all the fighting power it could muster. But the major did not force these civilians to join the battle, and he urged his soldiers to avoid taking risks. "Be careful of your lives," he said. " . . . do your duty coolly, determinedly and cautiously."

When Major Anderson refused the honor of firing the first Union shot, Captain Abner Doubleday eagerly accepted the task. The burly captain had none of Anderson's qualms about battling against his former countrymen. "I fully believed the contest was inevitable, and was not of our seeking," Doubleday explained. After months of impatiently watching his cautious commander, Doubleday happily ordered the gunners into action.

After two hours had passed without a sound from Sumter, some Southerners were beginning to wonder whether Anderson planned to surrender without a fight and ruin their chances for a glorious battle. The rebels cheered when they saw the first Union cannonball come hurling across the harbor. The effect of Captain Doubleday's shot did little to subdue their high spirits. The ball bounced harmlessly off the roof of the Confederate ironclad battery—a platform mounted with guns and shielded with metal bars.

For the next several hours, Doubleday launched a steady attack on the iron battery, while his fellow officers aimed at other targets around the harbor. But as the smoke from each shot cleared, the men were dismayed to realize that their cannonballs had barely dented the enemy's well-armored gun stations. The Union soldiers needed more powerful weapons—and the maddening fact was that these arms were available. However, the huge guns that could send hundred-pound balls smashing into the rebel barricades were lined up on the unprotected levels of the fort. Major Anderson had given

In the North, Major Robert Anderson became a hero for tirelessly defending his country against "southern traitors." Wrote one admirer to the major: "I will take the liberty of informing you . . . that you are today the most popular man in the nation."

his men strict orders to stay away from the open ramparts, where deadly Confederate shells were landing at a fierce rate.

For Private John Carmody, the idea of blasting the enemy with such splendid weapons was too tempting to ignore. Disobeying his commander's orders, he slipped away from his company and sneaked up the circular staircase that led to the ramparts. The heavy cannon aimed at Fort Moultrie were already loaded. With Confederate balls whistling by, the daredevil soldier dashed along the row of waiting guns and fired them one by one. "The contest was merely Carmody against the Confederate States," his friend Sergeant Chester later wrote, "and Carmody had to back down, not because he was beaten, but because he was unable, single-handedly to reload his guns."

At the sound of the big guns firing, Major Anderson must have wondered who was defying his orders. But there was a more serious problem to occupy his attention: Fort Sumter was running out of ammunition. By noon the supply of precious cartridge bags, which contained gunpowder charges needed for each shot, had dwindled to a small pile. Many of the workmen, who had turned pale when the shelling began, now offered their help. While some carried barrels of powder out to the gun decks, others busily sewed sheets and shirts into cartridge bags. Unfortunately, there were only six needles for sewing. As fast as the workmen could finish the bags, the soldiers loaded them in their cannon and blew them apart. As the supply of cartridges disappeared, Major Anderson had no choice but to limit his firing to six guns.

In the midst of this crisis, a shout rang out, convincing the Union soldiers that their problems were over. The relief ships had arrived! Out beyond the mouth of the harbor were two man-of-war vessels, barely visible through the haze of battle smoke. As the ships steamed closer, the soldiers rejoiced at the sight of the Union flags, and imagined how different the next twenty-four hours would be. They were certain that once darkness fell, the warships would land at Sumter, bringing more troops, ammunition, and all the fresh meat and vegetables they could eat. Then, at daybreak, the Union boys would make the rebels sorry they ever dared to challenge the power of the Stars and Stripes.

While a wave of hope swept through the fort, Captain Gustavus Fox was beginning to realize that his relief mission had gone terribly wrong. Seven other vessels had been scheduled to meet Captain Fox ten miles out of Charleston harbor on April 12. But when his steamer, the *Baltic*, arrived at the specified meeting place, only one other gunboat, the *Harriet Lane*, was anchored in the heavy seas. After three agonizing hours, another warship finally appeared. Although it meant disobeying orders from Washington, Captain Fox refused to drift aimlessly in the waves and wait for the rest of the fleet to arrive. Followed by the *Harriet Lane*, he ordered the *Baltic* to head toward Fort Sumter.

As the ships approached the harbor, Captain Fox was startled to hear the ominous thundering of cannon and see a shroud of smoke. He was too late. It would be nearly impossible for the two boats to reinforce Sumter without being crippled by Confederate gunfire. Burning with impatience, the captain settled down to wait for the missing ships of his expedition—four of which would never appear. As he learned much later, two of the vessels had been pushed off course by a storm, one had been called on another mission, and another had never even left its port.

After a few restless hours of sleep, the soldiers at Fort Sumter awoke to a dismal morning. The relief ships had not budged during the night. There they were, still bobbing up and down beyond the sandbar, as if their crews were on a sightseeing tour instead of a rescue operation. So once again, the troops ate salt pork for breakfast, then desperately tried to fend off the driving Confederate attack.

Putting up a good fight was becoming more and more difficult. The rebels had found a potent tactic for causing chaos in the Union fort. Before loading their cannon, the Confederates placed cannonballs in giant furnaces until they were red with heat. When fired, a "hot shot" could bury itself in the wooden barracks of the fort and eventually turn the area into a wall of flames. By ten o'clock in the morning on April 13, fires were already roaring through the passageways of Sumter. As soon as the men brought one blaze under control, another area broke into flames. To the rebels stationed around the harbor, Fort Sumter looked like an island of fire. But still the Union soldiers found a way to man their guns. The Confederates were so impressed by their enemy's deter-

Inside Fort Sumter, Confederate shells ripped off the top of the flagstaff and demolished the officers' quarters. When the Union banner fell during one tense moment of the attack, a brave lieutenant rushed through the blazing parade ground to save the flag, burning off his eyebrows in the rescue.

mination that they cheered whenever a Union shot came soaring over the water.

Meanwhile, the fire was inching dangerously close to the Sumter supply room where three hundred barrels of gunpowder were stored. Fearing an enormous explosion, Major Anderson ordered his men to move the kegs away from the blaze. With hot cinders and shells raining down around them, every available man—officers, soldiers, workmen, and musicians—frantically set to work. But it soon became clear that there were no safe places to store the powder. Major Anderson was forced to order his exhausted men to roll all but five barrels into the sea.

With more hot shot flying in at a steady rate, the smoke in the fort became too much to bear. It billowed through every corner, choking the soldiers and blinding the gunners' eyes. "It seemed impossible to escape suffocation," remembered Captain Doubleday. "Some lay down close to the ground, with handkerchiefs over their mouths. . . ." Others risked crawling out onto the open ledges of the fort for a gulp of clean air.

Even before Confederate messengers arrived at Fort Sumter, Major Anderson knew it was time to surrender. His fort stood in ruins. Most of the gunpowder was floating in the harbor; the workmen, who had run out of sheets, were using socks to sew cartridge bags. And Captain Fox was obviously not planning to send in more supplies anytime soon. Worst of all, the soldiers were weary and discouraged. Through more than thirty hours of bombardment, they had bravely defended the Union cause. Now Major Anderson could do nothing more than let them go home. When General Beauregard's aides arrived to work out the terms of surrender, Anderson agreed to evacuate Fort Sumter the next day—after his garrison had fired a one-hundred-gun salute to the ragged Union flag.

On the morning of the surrender, April 14, 1861, the citizens of Charleston flocked to the waterfront to witness the historic scene. Overnight the harbor had been transformed from a battleground to a festive marina of pleasure boats. Ferries, rafts, skiffs, and rowboats carried brightly dressed passengers to get a closer look at the fallen fort. From the banks of the city, many spectators could barely see the battered stronghold behind the clouds of smoke still pouring from its walls. But the view was not important. It was enough to know that in just a few hours, the Union forces would be marched back to northern territory where they belonged.

In the streets of Charleston, people celebrated wildly. Businesses closed, parades snaked through the city, and everywhere southern men gave victory speeches and toasted the Confederate cause. Mary Chesnut and two companions surveyed the merrymaking from an open carriage. "What a changed scene," wrote Mrs. Chesnut in her diary. "The very liveliest crowd I think I ever saw. Everybody talking at once. All glasses still turned on the grim old fort."

In the spring of 1861, it was this scene that represented the idea of war for many American people. During the bombardment

Confederates inspect the ramparts of Fort Sumter after the Union surrender. The powerful guns shown here, lined up along an unprotected level of the fort, were among those that Major Anderson instructed his soldiers not to fire.

of Fort Sumter, no soldiers had been killed on either side. And the battle did not leave a single scar on the graceful city of Charleston. To these Americans, war meant patriotism and parades. They believed it was a time when gallant officers, wearing red sashes, met to arrange the terms of battle—a time when the victors politely offered brandy to the losing side. When they thought of war, they imagined handsome young men in fine uniforms marching smartly back home after serving their country well.

As the nation sank deeper and deeper into civil war, Americans would realize that most of these ideas were pure fantasy. They would learn that war meant the destruction of their homes and the death of thousands of young men. By the end of the four-year struggle, many would have forgotten exactly what arguments first divided the North and the South. But in the spring of 1861, most Americans were glad to end their war of words and march off to settle their differences on the battlefield. ★

Glossary

abolitionist   a person who worked to end the practice of slavery in the United States

battery   a barrier set up to protect gunners and their weapons

Border Ruffians   the name given to rough Missouri frontiersmen who illegally invaded Kansas to pose as settlers from the territory and vote for proslavery candidates

compromise   a settlement of differences in which each side gives up some demands or makes sacrifices in order to reach an agreement

Confederate States of America   the alliance of eleven southern states that withdrew from the United States in 1860 and 1861. These states included Alabama, Arkansas, Florida, Georgia, Louisiana, Mississippi, North Carolina, South Carolina, Tennessee, Texas, and Virginia.

cotton gin   a machine used to remove the hard seeds from cotton fibers. The gin was invented by Eli Whitney in 1793

delegate   a person chosen to represent the wishes of a particular group

Democratic party   a major political group in the United States. During the Civil War era, members of the party believed that the states should control their own affairs without interference from the government in Washington, D.C.

federal   having to do with the union of states that recognized the authority of the central United States government based in Washington, D.C.

fugitive   a person who flees; a runaway

garrison   troops stationed in a fort or military post

immigrant   a person who settles permanently in a foreign country

Industrial Age   the period when machines and power tools replaced hand tools, making it possible to produce goods on a large scale. In America, the Industrial Age reached its peak during the 1850s.

legislature   a group of people given the responsibility and power to make laws for a country or a state

overseer   a supervisor or foreman who watches over and directs the work of others

parapet   a low wall along the edge of a fort's roof designed to protect soldiers from enemy fire

plantation   a large estate or farm where crops were tended by slaves

population   the total number of people living in a particular area

Republican party   a major political group in the United States organized in 1854 to oppose the spread of slavery

secession   the withdrawal from membership in an organization or group

Underground Railroad   a secret system set up by opponents of slavery to help runaway slaves from the South escape to the free states and Canada

Union   another name for the United States of America, used especially during the Civil War. Sixteen out of thirty-three states remained loyal to the Union during the war.

Bibliography

★ ★ ★ ★

Basler, Roy, ed. *The Collected Works of Abraham Lincoln.* New Brunswick, N.J.: Rutgers University Press, 1955.

Conrad, Earl. *Harriet Tubman.* New York: Eriksson, 1970.

Davis, William C., ed. *Brother Against Brother: The War Begins.* Alexandria, Va.: Time-Life Books (Time-Life American Civil War Series, Vol. 1), 1983.

—————. *Shadows of the Storm (The Image of War: 1861–1865, Vol. 1).* New York: Doubleday & Company, 1981.

Doubleday, Abner. *Reminiscences of Forts Sumter and Moultrie in 1860–61.* New York: Harper & Brothers, 1876.

Eaton, Clement. *Henry Clay and the Art of American Politics.* Boston: Little, Brown & Company, 1957.

Hamilton, Virginia. *Anthony Burns: The Defeat and Triumph of a Fugitive Slave Law.* New York: Knopf, 1988.

Keller, Allan. *Thunder at Harper's Ferry.* Englewood Cliffs, N.J.: Prentice-Hall, 1958.

Ketchem, Richard, ed. *The American Heritage Picture History of the Civil War.* New York: American Heritage Publishing Company, 1960.

McCurdy, Frances Lea. *Stump, Bar, and Pulpit: Speechmaking on the Missouri Frontier.* Columbia: University of Missouri Press, 1969.

McPherson, James M. *Battle Cry of Freedom: The Civil War Era.* New York: Oxford University Press, 1988.

Nichols, Alice. *Bleeding Kansas.* New York: Oxford University Press, 1954.

Northup, Solomon. *Twelve Years a Slave.* Baton Rouge: Louisiana State University Press, 1968.

Oates, Stephen B. *To Purge This Land With Blood: A Biography of John Brown.* New York: Harper Torchbooks, 1970.

——————. *With Malice Toward None: The Life of Abraham Lincoln.* New York: Harper & Row, 1977.

Osofsky, Gilbert, ed. *Puttin' On Ole Massa.* New York: Harper & Row, 1969.

Pierce, Edward. *Memoir and Letters of Charles Sumner.* Boston: Roberts Brothers, 1893.

Russell, William Howard. *My Diary North and South.* New York: Harper & Brothers, 1954.

Storey, Moorfield. *Charles Sumner.* Boston: Houghton Mifflin Company, 1900.

Swanberg, W. A. *First Blood: The Story of Fort Sumter.* New York: Charles Scribner's Sons, 1957.

Van Deusen, Glyndon G. *The Life of Henry Clay.* Boston: Little, Brown & Company, 1937.

Washington, Booker T. *Up From Slavery.* New York: Doubleday, 1901.

Woodward, C. Vann, ed. *Mary Chesnut's Civil War.* New Haven: Yale University Press, 1981.

Manuscripts

Robert Anderson Papers, Library of Congress.

Samuel Crawford Papers, Library of Congress.

Theodore Talbot Papers, Library of Congress.

Index

★ ★ ★ ★

Page numbers in *italics* refer to illustrations

Picture Credits

★ ★ ★ ★

The photographs in this book are from the following sources and are used with their permission:

Chicago Historical Society • page 93

Fort Sumter National Monument, Sullivan's Island, S.C. • page 84

Kennedy Galleries, New York, N.Y. • page 12

Library of Congress, Washington, D.C. • pages ii, 3, 6, 8-9, 14, 18, 20, 25, 26, 29, 32, 34, 40, 43, 45, 47, 49, 50, 54, 57, 64, 66, 70, 74, 76, 79, 81, 82, 86

Museum of the Confederacy, Richmond, Va. • page 83

National Archives, Washington, D.C. • pages 10, 15, 23, 24, 28, 30, 37, 44, 55, 61, 88, 91

The New-York Historical Society • pages 19, 22

New York Public Library • page 62

U.S. Army Military History Institute, Carlisle Barracks, Pa. • page 16

Yale University Art Gallery (Mabel Brady Garvan Collection), New Haven, Conn. • pages 58–59